The Peopling of Bandelier

The publication of this book was made possible by generous gifts
from the Friends of Bandelier, Maggie and Christian Andersson
for the Loretto Chapel of Santa Fe,
and William S. Cowles.

The Peopling

New Insights from the Archaeology of

A School of American Research
Popular Southwestern Archaeology Book

# of Bandelier

the Pajarito Plateau

Edited by Robert P. Powers

School of American Research Press
Santa Fe, New Mexico

School of American Research Press
Post Office Box 2188
Santa Fe, New Mexico 87504-2188
www.sarweb.org

Director: James F. Brooks
Executive Editor: Catherine Cocks
Developmental and Illustration Editor: Willow Roberts Powers
Copy Editor: Jane Kepp
Design and Production: Cynthia Dyer
Maps: Molly O'Halloran
Proofreader: Ellen Cavalli
Indexer: Catherine Fox
Printed in China by C&C Offset Printing

Library of Congress Cataloging-in-Publication Data

The peopling of Bandelier : new insights from the archaeology of the
Pajarito Plateau / edited by Robert P. Powers.
p. cm.
"A School of American Research popular southwestern archaeology book."
Includes bibliographical references and index.
ISBN 1-930618-53-0 (pbk. : alk. paper) — ISBN 1-930618-67-0 (cloth : alk. paper)
1. Pueblo Indians—New Mexico—Pajarito Plateau—Antiquities.
2. Pueblo Indians—New Mexico—Bandelier National Monument—Antiquities.
3. Excavations (Archaeology)—New Mexico—Pajarito Plateau.
4. Excavations (Archaeology)—New Mexico—Bandelier National Monument.
5. Bandelier National Monument (N.M.)—History.
6. Bandelier National Monument (N.M.)—Antiquities. 7. Pajarito Plateau (N.M.)—Antiquities.
I. Powers, Robert P., 1952-

E99.P9P395 2004   978.9'57—dc22
2004023520

Cover photograph (front): Frijoles Canyon. View from Tyuonyi Pueblo to Talus House, courtesy David G. Noble, photographer..
Cover photograph (back): Atilano Montoya, expert hunter and uncle of Julian Martinez, Plate 13, 29th Bureau of American
Ethnology Annual Report (1907-1908).

Contents

Illustrations

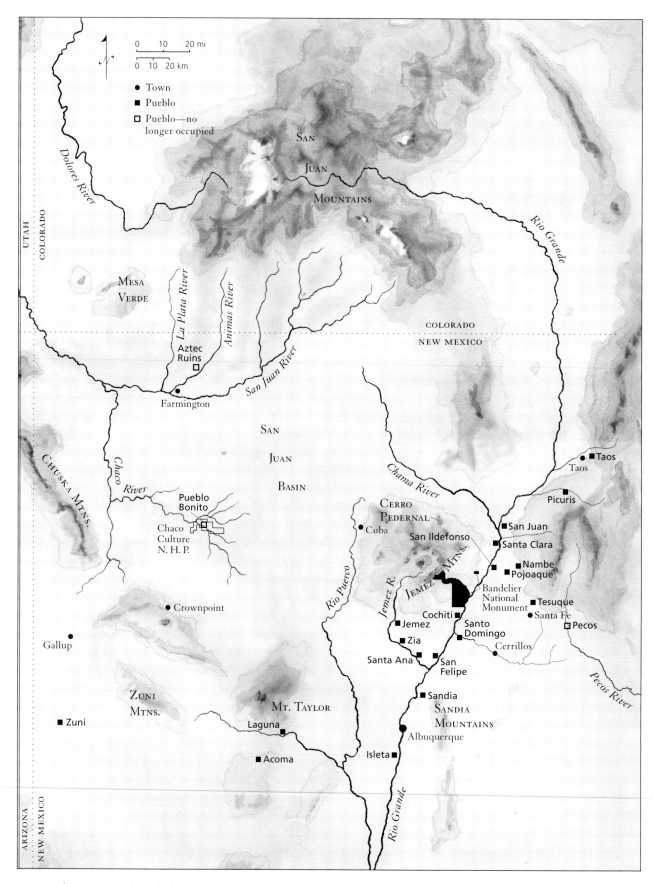

Map 1. The eastern Colorado Plateau and northern Rio Grande Valley.

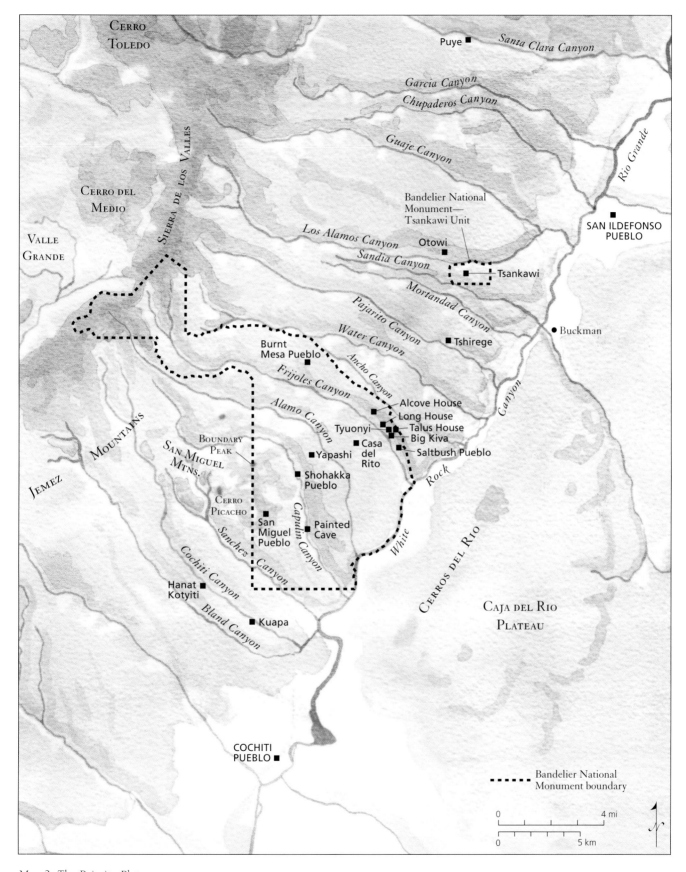

Map 2. The Pajarito Plateau.

Acknowledgments

During a staff meeting at Bandelier National Monument nearly twenty years ago, I naively promised to prepare a popular book on the archaeology of Bandelier. Eveyone at the table agreed that it was at last possible to write a book using the trove of data that James Hill's Pajarito Archaeological Research Project, Timothy Kohler's Bandelier Archaeological Excavation Project, and my own project, the Bandelier Archaeological Survey, were producing.

Robert P. Powers

Some of the people at that meeting are now dead, and almost everyone else has moved on, but two of the people who were there share responsibility for this book. Ed Greene, then chief of interpretation at Bandelier, was our most ardent supporter. More than anyone else, Ed realized that our work could transform the park's prehistory. Alas, archaeology moves at a glacial pace, and Ed had gone on to a new assignment before our work was complete. Nonetheless, his commitment to telling Bandelier's story inspired this book, and I sincerely hope we have finally written something he would find useful. Rory Gauthier, now park archaeologist at Bandelier, has made the archaeology of the Pajarito his life's work. In addition to contributing as an author, he advised me over the course of two years on almost every aspect of this book.

I would like to thank the School of American Research Press, and especially James F. Brooks, its director, for recognizing the need for a popular book on Bandelier written by archaeologists and for providing enthusiastic support at every step of the way. Dorothy Hoard, president for the Board of Trustees of the Friends of Bandelier, is the Pajarito's best friend; she has worked tirelessly for the last thirty years to protect and preserve her beloved plateau. Under her guidance, the Friends have provided essential financial support for this book, which I gratefully acknowledge. Through an agreement crafted by Robert Eaton, of the Office of the Solicitor, the Friends will receive a share of the royalties from the sales of this book.

At the National Park Service, I thank my boss, James Bradford, for allowing me to work on this book as part of my National Park Service duties. At Bandelier National Monument, superintendent Darlene Koontz, chief of resources James Mack, and chief of interpretation Lynne Dominy all strongly supported our efforts.

I especially want to thank the contributors for willingly sharing their knowledge, expertise, and enthusiasm for Pajaritan archaeology and for patiently enduring the many drafts and revisions required to bring the book to its final form. Michael R. Walsh and I would like to thank Genevieve Head for providing feedback and ideas on Mike's chapter and for help in selecting the chapter illustrations. Myron Gonzales, director of the cultural resources program at San Ildefonso Pueblo, and Sam Arquero, governor of Cochiti Pueblo, were instrumental in arranging the participation of Pueblo elders Julian Martinez and Joseph Henry Suina. I thank both Julian and Joseph for sharing their views of the Puebloan world.

Catherine Cocks, executive editor at the School of American Research Press, is the calm, resourceful, and realistic editor every author hopes for, and Jane Kepp lent her usual editorial acumen as well. Molly O'Halloran and Cynthia Dyer expertly drafted the maps and line illustrations. David Grant Noble graciously took the cover and frontispiece photographs during two memorable trips to Bandelier.

Addison Doty took many of the fine artifact photos. Tomas Jaehn, of the Palace of the Governors History Library and Archives, made invaluable archival photographs available. Bandelier National Monument, the National Park Service's Intermountain Support Office, the Indian Arts Research Center of the School of American Research, the Office of Archeological Studies of the Museum of New Mexico, Los Alamos National Laboratory, Santa Fe National Forest, the Smithsonian Institution, the Museum of Indian Arts and Culture, and Paul Schuman graciously allowed us to photograph objects in their collections. Cynthia Dyer, of the School of American Research, designed the book, Ellen Cavalli proofread it, and Catherine Fox prepared the index.

Finally, I thank my wife, Willow, for agreeing to be the developmental editor and for providing wise counsel, criticism, and support throughout the book's genesis.

A Chronology for Bandelier National Monument and the Pajarito Plateau

9500	Paleoindian hunters and gatherers arrive on the plateau, just before end of last ice age
6000	Archaic hunters and gatherers on the plateau
1200	Maize grown at Jemez Cave

CE (of the common era)

1150	Puebloan settlers move onto the plateau, building small hamlets
1200–1250	Population expands rapidly through immigration
1250–1290	Population declines during period of extended drought
1290–1325	Population peaks as more immigrants arrive; first large pueblos are constructed; territories are established and glaze ware introduced
1325–1440	Number of people declines and dry intervals become more frequent; villages grow larger; village-wide religious ceremonies unify communities
1440–1525	Frijoles cavate pueblos are constructed and Frijoles population peaks
1525–1550	Mesa-top villages in Bandelier are abandoned; number of people in Frijoles Canyon declines
1540–1541	Coronado expedition bypasses the Pajarito
1550–1600	Drought in 1570s–1590s results in abandonment of Pajarito by 1600
1598–1610	Juan de Oñate establishes first Spanish settlement at San Juan Pueblo; Santa Fe is founded
1680–1692	Pueblo Revolt; Pueblos seek refuge on the Pajarito during Spanish reconquest
1846	United States occupies New Mexico and proclaims it a territory
1912	New Mexico achieves statehood
1916	President Woodrow Wilson establishes Bandelier National Monument

Picture Credits

The Peopling of Bandelier

Figure 1.1. Adolph Bandelier and his wife, Fanny.

A Grand and Isolated Place

Robert P. Powers

Some 125 years ago an intrepid Southwestern ethnologist and historian named Adolph Bandelier scribbled an entry in his journal, describing with amazement a canyon filled with Pueblo ruins and cave dwellings in a remote part of northern New Mexico:

> The grandest thing I ever saw. A magnificent growth of pines, *encina*, *alamos* and towering cliffs, of pumice or volcanic tuff, exceedingly friable. The cliffs are vertical on the north side, and their bases are, for a length as yet unknown to me, used as dwellings both from the inside and, by inserting the roof poles, for stories outside. It is of the highest interest. There are some of one, two, and three stories.... Aside from the caves, there are ruins of a large pueblo, immense *estufas*, round towers of two stories, etc.

Bandelier's journal entry became the first written record of the rugged beauty of isolated Frijoles Canyon and its impressive but enigmatic archaeological sites. In the century since his first visit, much has changed. A trip to Frijoles no longer requires a two-day mule ride, and the canyon is now part of Bandelier National Monument. Each year more than three hundred thousand visitors descend into the canyon to inspect the ruins and, on hot summer days, dabble their feet in Frijoles Creek. What has not changed is the way visitors react. Their first glimpse of the canyon still provokes the same mixture of surprise, awe, and curiosity that Bandelier expressed in his diary.

Despite the extraordinary wealth of archaeologi-cal sites on the Pajarito Plateau—the volcanic tuff tableland dissected by Frijoles and other canyons—relatively little archaeology has been done there. Because of this, the story of Bandelier National Monument and the surrounding plateau has remained, as writers love to say, "shrouded in mystery." Fortunately, an abundance of new, innovative research, much of it conducted by the authors of this book, has begun to unveil a complex human story that is as singular and thought-provoking as that of better-known Chaco Canyon and Mesa Verde. It is made all the more compelling by the lateness of its telling. It is both a new story and an ancient tale, and it is as grand as any Bandelier could have imagined.

Idyllic but Unpredictable

Part of the seductive power of the Pajarito Plateau lies in its spectacular volcanic landscape. Wedged between the rim of the Jemez Mountains and the Rio Grande, the plateau is a nine-hundred-foot layer of solidified volcanic ash, or tuff, deposited more than a million years ago by the explosion of the Valles Caldera. Within its roughly 220-square-mile expanse, the plateau ranges from 5,500 to over 8,000 feet in elevation. A dozen deep canyons cut it into long, sloping mesas (see plate 1). A few canyons with permanent streams, such as Frijoles, are oases that nourish water-loving plants and animals that otherwise could not survive.

The sheer tuff cliffs of the canyons hold the remains of hundreds of cliff-face apartments that Puebloan people excavated into the soft rock. In

Figure 1.2. Cavate rooms in the north wall of Frijoles Canyon, seen from Tyuonyi Pueblo.

Frijoles Canyon these dwellings, known as "cavate rooms" or just "cavates," accompanied the nearby village of Tyuonyi to form a prehistoric community that spread along the canyon for over a mile. Frijoles Canyon is so impressive that many visitors come away convinced that the canyons must have been the focus of human life on the plateau. In fact, during their first three centuries there the Puebloans lived not in the canyons but on the mesa tops, abandoning them only when they were no longer capable of sustaining agriculture.

Because the Pajaritans lived both on the mesas and in the canyons, it is hard to walk anywhere on the Pajarito Plateau without spotting broken pieces of pottery or stone flakes—or, more prosaically, rusting cans and shards of glass—all enduring fragments of the plateau's nearly twelve-thousand-year human history. The Pajarito holds an estimated ten thousand archaeological sites, from nearly invisible scatters of artifacts to immense Puebloan villages. These remains offer gritty evidence of the inventive ways in which humans used this landscape and how it shaped their lives. Indeed, what is most fascinating about the Pajarito is how successfully its people have faced the difficulties and uncertainties of making a living in a drought-prone and always unpredictable environment. These challenges were most ingeniously met by Puebloan farmers who made the plateau their home during the late prehistoric period.

Reinventing Pueblo Life in a New Landscape

The Puebloan farmers who colonized the Pajarito Plateau in the late 1100s and 1200s were desert-smart survivors who had been victims of their own success. Immigrants from Chaco Canyon, Mesa Verde, and the San Juan River area, they carried with them the distilled wisdom earned during seven centuries of farming-based village life in the northern Southwest. They were masters at coaxing crops from poor, parched soils and at supplementing their harvests with hunted game and edible wild plants. They were also wary, chastened refugees of the vast network of great-house communities that covered much of the eastern Colorado Plateau between 1000 and 1300 CE. Beginning with Chaco great houses in the early 1000s and ending with Mesa Verde commu-

nities in the late 1200s, these elaborate ceremonial and residential centers collapsed in a tangled web of drought, internal dissension, and violence.

Settling on the Pajarito gave the refugees a chance to start anew and learn from old mistakes. We might suppose that many of the immigrants vowed never again to live in large villages or heed the instructions of elite religious leaders. During the 1100s and early 1200s, little happened to challenge these resolutions, but as thousands more immigrants poured onto the plateau in the late 1200s, it became increasingly clear that organized communities and wise political and religious leaders were needed to apportion and protect agricultural land and wild foods, establish food reserves, and promote cooperation and concord among people with different backgrounds and languages. How the Puebloans reinvented village life to meet the special demands of the Pajarito landscape—and the consequences of their actions—forms the plateau's most compelling story.

Telling the Pajarito Story

In the chapters that follow, my colleagues use findings from recent archaeological research to address this and related themes. Better archaeological evidence collected during the last thirty years makes it possible to ask and answer increasingly sophisticated questions. The new evidence grew out of three important investigations. First, members of the eight-year-long Pajarito Archaeological Research Project, directed by James N. Hill of the University of California, Los Angeles, surveyed for sites across the Pajarito and excavated some of them. A second study, the Bandelier Archaeological Survey, was prompted by a lack of comprehensive, accurate information about sites in Bandelier National Monument. Under my direction, project staff recorded valuable data on nearly two thousand prehistoric and historic sites. Third, Timothy A. Kohler's Bandelier Archaeological Excavation Project greatly expanded the reach of the survey by excavating at six sites together spanning more than four hundred years of ancestral Pueblo life. Stimulated in part by these studies, researchers continue to survey, excavate, and preserve sites in Bandelier and around Los Alamos National Laboratory.

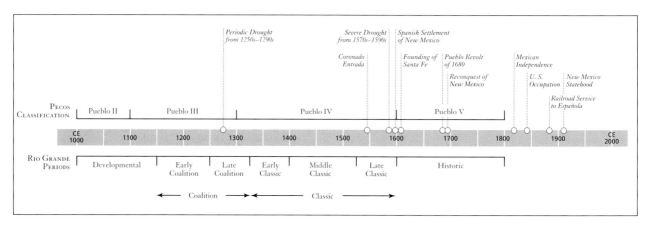

Figure 1.3. Archaeological time periods and major events in the northern Rio Grande region.

Because it is difficult to summarize all the research that has been conducted, we chose topics for this book that illuminate key aspects of the Pajarito story. Most of the chapters are focused on the Puebloans who lived on the plateau between 1150 and 1550 or 1600 CE, but the authors also describe human use of the plateau during the earlier Paleoindian and Archaic periods and during later historic times.

Archaeologists commonly divide the Pueblo era in the northern Rio Grande region into two cultural periods, the Coalition (1150–1325) and the Classic (1325–1550/1600). During the Coalition period, Puebloan immigrants arrived on the Pajarito Plateau and built hundreds of small, mostly short-lived settlements. Rapid population growth during the 1200s and early 1300s led to competition for land and food. During the Classic period, people constructed large villages, new religious beliefs and ceremonies emerged, and social and political life became more complex as Puebloans adapted to communal living and a drier climate.

Although much of the Pajarito Plateau today appears wild and untouched by humans, this is far from the case. To those trained to see its clues, the landscape bears the subtle traces of centuries of environmental and climatic change, as well as human use. In chapter 2, ecologist Craig Allen introduces the environment and climate of the plateau since the end of the last ice age. He describes the geology, soils, plant and animal life, and rainfall patterns to which the plateau's people had to adapt, as well as the significant alterations

people in turn worked on the plateau.

Paleoindian hunters, who arrived at the close of the Pleistocene geological epoch, were the first humans to use the Pajarito Plateau, from about 9500 to 6000 BCE—though the only evidence of their presence is the occasional finely made spear or dart point. Warming temperatures and the extinction of many big game mammals brought an end to the Paleoindian lifestyle and the beginning of a long era known as the Archaic, from about 6000 BCE to 500 CE. Archaic people, like their Paleoindian predecessors, lived in small, mobile groups that ranged across the landscape, hunting mammals and foraging for edible plants in a carefully scheduled yearly round tuned to the seasonal availability of each plant or animal. In chapter 3, Bradley Vierra describes the unique challenges of Paleoindian and Archaic life on the plateau. As he emphasizes, there is much to envy in a hunting and gathering lifestyle. For one thing, most hunter-gatherers probably did not work as hard as later farming people. And because their diet was highly varied and low in fats, Archaic people enjoyed better health than many of us do today.

Coalition-Period Farmers

When the first Puebloan farmers arrived around 1150 CE, the Pajarito Plateau had been little used for more than five hundred years. The colonists built small masonry and adobe pueblos that archaeologists characterize as hamlets, and they established fields watered by rainfall. Population ballooned through the early 1200s as more immigrants arrived, many of them probably from around Mesa Verde and the

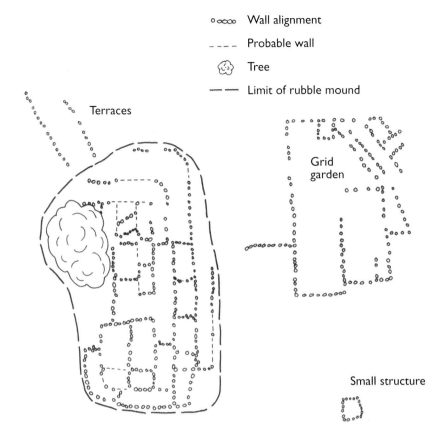

Wall alignment
Probable wall
Tree
Limit of rubble mound

Terraces

Grid
garden

Small structure

Figure 1.4. Plan of a Coalition-period hamlet.

San Juan River. Most settlements appear to have been used for no more than a generation, probably because nearby resources, including agricultural land, were exhausted. As people abandoned old settlements, they founded new ones in virgin locations, a cycle that was repeated for the next 175 years.

Because depleted farmland had to be fallowed, Puebloan immigrants found themselves increasingly in competition with one another for new land. Good farmland was never abundant on the plateau, and because summer rains were unpredictable, farmers became adept at producing crops under difficult conditions. In chapter 4, Rory Gauthier and Cynthia Herhahn describe the ingenious strategies Pajaritan farmers developed as population increased, land became scarcer, soils were depleted, and climate became drier.

The Pajaritans' growing dependence on corn, beans, and squash during the Coalition period, together with their domestication of turkeys, sug-

gests that they were depleting the wild game in their territory. Relying on domesticated plants and animals increased their control over the food supply, but it also sparked far-reaching changes in the Puebloan diet. In chapter 5, Kari Schmidt and Meredith Matthews describe how late Archaic and Puebloan foods changed over the course of four thousand years on the plateau. Drawing on painstaking studies of plant remains and animal bones, the two address a crucial question: How and why did diet change as the plateau's inhabitants increased in number and became more dependent on agriculture?

A harbinger of coming agricultural hardships arrived around 1250 CE in the form of a serious drought that continued through the late 1290s. At Mesa Verde, the later part of this infamous period, popularly known as the "Great Drought," saw a total depopulation of the region. On the Pajarito, population dropped precipitously, but after 1300, climatic conditions improved and it boomed again, reaching a peak of nearly four thousand people in what is now Bandelier National Monument alone. Many of these people undoubtedly came from the Mesa Verde and San Juan River areas. Until that time, most Pajaritan hamlets had sheltered no more than a few families, but after 1350, large pueblos, each housing several hundred residents, began to appear.

Classic-Period Villagers
How and why villages develop has been a subject of intense interest to archaeologists in recent years. In chapter 6, Tineke Van Zandt describes Puebloan villages and the settlement landscape they created on the Pajarito Plateau. She explains how the

Figure 1.5. A petroglyph panel on a basalt boulder in White Rock Canyon, depicting deer, snakes, and a shield.

development of large communities might have reduced competition for land, provided food in times of need, and promoted cooperation and unity among village members.

Clues to a renewed importance of religious beliefs and ceremonies involving entire villages during the Classic period are preserved in rock art near some Pajarito villages. In chapter 7, Marit Munson describes the plateau's abundant and ever-perplexing petroglyphs and pictographs. She finds that before the early 1300s, rock art frequently displayed war-related themes. After that date, the imagery shifted to religious scenes, including depictions of supernatural beings in human form.

The war symbolism in rock art coincided with the boom in immigration and the construction of the first villages, some of which, such as Burnt Mesa Pueblo on the northern edge of Bandelier National Monument, assert a distinctly defensive character. Competition over territory and resources was a fact of life on the plateau in the late 1200s and early 1300s, and tension manifested itself in the creation of village and ethnic boundaries. Interestingly, the most visible boundary centered on Frijoles Canyon.

Archaeologists deduced the existence of this boundary in part by studying stone tools. Puebloans on the Pajarito Plateau used three kinds of stone—obsidian, basalt, and chert—for almost all the stone implements they manufactured, yet each of these materials outcrops in only a few places. In chapter 8, Michael Walsh shows that each of these materials was initially used by people living nearest to its sources, but unaccountably, the pattern was disrupted in the Frijoles Canyon area in the late 1200s. The change in people's uses of different types of stone appears to reflect the imposition of social constraints on raw material collecting on either side of Frijoles Canyon. What is most tantalizing about this apparent archaeological boundary is that it closely corresponds to a boundary described by Keres and Tewa people in their oral traditions. These two Pueblo groups, who now live in the Rio Grande Valley and who are named for the languages they speak, not only identify the Pajarito as their ancestral homeland but also mark Frijoles Canyon as the dividing line between their historic territories.

The Frijoles boundary acquires another dimension from studies of pottery, the most common artifact on the Pajarito Plateau. Distinguished by its thick, shiny, lead-based paint, a new type of ceramic known as glaze ware became the most common household pottery south of Frijoles Canyon in the 1300s. North of Frijoles, a locally made pottery called biscuit ware predominated. Although both kinds of vessels saw everyday use and were widely traded, each eventually served a less obvious role: it became a social marker. Like chert and basalt tools, each of the two wares stops at Frijoles Canyon. But was that always the case? In chapter 9, James Vint shows that the boundary between the wares moved northward over time, reaching

Figure 1.6. A deeply worn prehistoric trail near Tsankawi Pueblo.

Frijoles in the early 1400s. He suggests that the spread of the two wares was a sign of emerging ethnic territories and widening trade networks.

Although Frijoles Canyon served as a boundary, it appears not to have formed a barrier. People to the north and south of it continued to trade with one another, traveling over a plateau-wide network of trails. Clearly visible where they were worn into the exposed tuff, these narrow bedrock paths were created by heavy foot traffic and intentional shaping. In chapter 10, James Snead describes the trails, the features found with them, where they go, and what they tell us about plateau community relations.

By 1450, in apparent response to a new and prolonged cycle of dry weather, population on the Pajarito declined further. Many people left altogether; others moved into canyons on the plateau with permanent water. In Frijoles Canyon, which was virtually unoccupied before 1300, population grew throughout the 1400s and peaked around 1500 at an estimated eight hundred people. This community, including Tyuonyi Pueblo, its supersize ceremonial building, known as Big Kiva, and the cavate pueblos along the north wall of the canyon, was one of the

largest on the Pajarito. Because cavate rooms were dug into the cliffs, their interior features—hearths, storage niches, anchors for weaving looms, wall plaster, and painted murals—are often beautifully preserved. In chapter 11, Angelyn Bass Rivera describes the cavates and the way they were furnished. She also weighs in on a long-standing question: Were cavate pueblos used differently from ordinary pueblos?

How long the Frijoles community remained vibrant is a question still unresolved, although tree-ring dates and time-diagnostic potsherds suggest that its population diminished after 1550. What caused the Pueblo people to leave the plateau remains uncertain, too, but it seems likely that their departure reflected both growing environmental challenges—depletion of game and edible plants, exhaustion of soils, increasingly dry weather—and the inability of village leaders to solve those problems. In chapter 12, Robert Preucel recounts one of several oral histories charting the Keresans' pilgrimage from Frijoles across the southern Pajarito Plateau. From the Keresan perspective, why villages were abandoned is less important than the villages themselves and the sequence in which the people lived in them. As Preucel emphasizes, oral traditions interweave historical narratives with myths and moral instruction.

Just Off the Map

After the late 1500s, the Pajarito Plateau saw little human activity for three hundred years. Both Keres and Tewa people, now living along the Rio Grande, maintained strong practical and spiritual ties with their ancestral homeland, using it for hunting and gathering and as a place for ceremonies. During the Spanish colonial and Mexican periods (1598–1846), the Pajarito was a dimly perceived wilderness, known mainly as a refuge for raiding nomads and livestock rustlers. In the later half of the 1800s, action surged there again as Hispanic and Pueblo shepherds introduced large flocks of sheep. Logging camps went up, too, and for a time, several mining camps flourished. In a few places homesteaders tried their hands at farming. Prospects for mining, logging, and herding waned as the economy weakened around the turn of the century, and

Figure 1.7. Shepherds with their flock in the Jemez Mountains, about 1935.

plateau farmers and ranchers eventually found themselves displaced by the federal government. In chapter 13, Monica Smith describes the startling transformation of the Pajarito from remote Pueblo homeland to host of the nation's premier nuclear weapons research laboratory.

One of the more recent permutations of the modern world to arrive on the Pajarito Plateau has been archaeology. Unsurprisingly, the impressive Classic-period villages such as Tyuonyi and Long House in Frijoles Canyon and Puye in Santa Clara Canyon to the north were among the first to be excavated. By current standards, the early investigations left much to be desired, but they proved crucial in establishing archaeology as a discipline and educating the public about its importance. In chapter 14, James Snead introduces us to early archaeology on the plateau through the *Rito de los Frijoles Gazette*, a handwritten newsletter issued during the 1910 and 1911 Frijoles field seasons. Produced by staff and students for their own amusement, it provides an intimate and often humorous view of life in an archaeological field camp nearly one hundred years ago.

Although we have learned much about the people of the Pajarito since Adolph Bandelier's first visit, much more remains to be discovered. What we know and hope to learn is summarized in chapter 15 by Timothy Kohler. Our final essay, presented in chapter 16, is drawn from a taped interview with two respected Pueblo elders, Joseph H. Suina of Cochiti Pueblo and Julian Martinez of San Ildefonso Pueblo. They close the volume by providing modern Keres and Tewa perspectives, respectively, on their ancestral homeland. Their reflections and observations on Puebloan life remind us that knowledge, whether scientific or traditional, is our most precious cultural artifact.

Figure 1.8. Pueblo excavators at Tyuonyi Pueblo, about 1910.

Robert P. Powers directed the Bandelier Archaeological
Survey and is an archaeologist with the National Park
Service in Santa Fe.

Figure 2.1. Pictograph of an elk in Painted Cave. Elk had vanished from the Pajarito Plateau by 1900 but were reintroduced midcentury.

A Thousand Years in the Life of a Landscape

Craig D. Allen

People have lived in the Jemez Mountains since at least the end of the last ice age, about eleven thousand years ago. Human cultures have changed much since then, and so has this landscape—people and nature have strongly influenced each other here. The magnitude of change has been particularly striking over the past thousand years or so, as human populations have ebbed and flowed and expanded along with their economies and ecosystems. How has the landscape around modern Bandelier National Monument evolved during this time, and how were people involved?

In the Southwest, scientists use many techniques to understand environmental change. They study growth rings from ancient gnarled trees, pollen and charcoal deposited in lakes and bogs, plant remains preserved in prehistoric packrat nests in dry rocky shelters, animal bones excavated from archaeological sites and caves, the patterns of landforms and soils, and even old written documents and photographs. Together these lines of evidence can be used to paint a fairly clear picture of how the Pajarito Plateau has changed since the end of the last ice age.

Geology, Landforms, and Soils

Bandelier National Monument sits on the southeastern flank of a huge volcanic landmass, the Jemez Mountains, overlooking the Rio Grande. The river is an ancient one, flowing down the trench of a rift valley where the earth has been pulling apart for millions of years, fostering volcanism along the valley's cracked margins. Massive eruptions about 1.2 million years ago explosively ejected seventy cubic miles of ash from the volcanic heart of the Jemez, causing the volcano's emptied-out core to collapse and creating the bowl of the Valles Caldera. The ash fell like a skirt around the margins of the Jemez Mountains and solidified into many rock layers, collectively up to nine hundred feet thick, known as the Bandelier Tuff. The Pajarito Plateau sits on this tuff skirt in the eastern Jemez Mountains, between the Rio Grande at about 5,400 feet in elevation and the higher peaks that rim the caldera at more than 10,000 feet.

Over the past million years or so, water draining toward the Rio Grande from the high caldera rim has carved many steep-walled canyons into the plateau, creating its distinctive landscape of elongated mesas and canyons. This deep canyon and mesa topography characterizes the entire Pajarito Plateau, including most of Bandelier National Monument, although north of Frijoles Canyon the canyons tend to be shallower, with broader valley floors.

This terrain has been home to many people over the millennia. Paleoindian, Archaic, and Puebloan knappers were all attracted by its variety of high-quality stone for making tools. Abundant deposits of dark volcanic glass—obsidian—outcrop in many parts of the Jemez Mountains. For thousands of years people quarried beautifully fine-textured basalt for tool making from an outcrop in present-day Bandelier near the mouth of Lummis Canyon. Cerro Pedernal ("flint peak"), in the northern Jemez Mountains, is one of several significant chert sources, and it, too, has been quarried for millennia.

Nodules of Pedernal chert are exposed in eroding gravels in the lower canyons of the northern Pajarito Plateau and sometimes turn up along the Rio Grande at Bandelier. Also found locally along the Rio Grande are cobbles of very hard crystalline rocks such as granite and quartzite, washed down from the Sangre de Cristo Mountains and other upstream sources.

Soils are alive. They vary from place to place, developing from the action of climate and vegetation on barren sediments and rock. Their suitability for agriculture also varies across a landscape like Bandelier's. Early farmers must have learned quickly the important differences—in soil moisture, soil fertility, and length of growing season—between upland mesa tops and drainages, canyon side slopes, and canyon bottoms. Slope steepness, slope direction (north or south facing), soil depth, and soil texture also greatly affect agricultural potential. On the mesa tops of the plateau, many soils are more than one hundred thousand years old, formed largely during the colder and wetter climate of the last ice age. These are well-developed soils with lots of clay, products of the breakdown of tuff and the accumulation of windblown dust through the ages. Deep, rich soils have developed in patches of coarse-textured pumice left on local mesas by the last volcanic "burps" from the Jemez, the El Cajete eruptions of fifty thousand years ago. With their protective mulching layer of pumice gravel, which absorbs and retains water, these became key agricultural soils for ancestral Puebloan farmers.

Dry and Variable Climate Is the Norm

For most of the last two million years the Earth has existed under ice age conditions. In the Southwest this meant a colder climate with wetter winters than those of the present. Mountain glaciers formed on the Sangre de Cristo peaks above Santa Fe, and in the Jemez Mountains, lower in elevation than the Sangres, near-glacial conditions prevailed. This glacial climate supported vegetation and wildlife patterns very different from those seen today. The last glacial period ended about eleven thousand years ago, when the Earth rather abruptly moved into a warmer pattern. The first known people to enter the Southwest did so shortly before this tran-

sition. From pollen and plant remains in ancient sediments and packrat nests we can tell that by about eight thousand years ago the key features of our modern climate were well established in this region.

The overall climate of the Jemez Mountains today is described as a semiarid continental climate. This means that growing plants are often stressed by lack of water and that cold temperatures prevent plant growth most of the year. There are distinct seasonal changes in moisture and temperature. Most moisture comes in the form of winter snow and summer rain, and dry, windy springs and dry fall weather are typical. Winter snows come from storm systems moving in the jet stream, coming off the Pacific Ocean. The spring drought is usually broken in early July by the onset of the summer "monsoon" season, when moisture from the Gulfs of Mexico and California enters the Southwest. Thunderstorms build up almost daily over the mountains and then move out erratically over adjoining lowlands. Nights are cool and days sunny most of the year. The daily cloud buildup of the summer thunderstorms cools down the early summer heat. On the Pajarito Plateau the growing season lasts about five months, from May through September.

The average conditions I have just described, however, vary a great deal from one local landscape to another. The high Jemez Mountains receive about three times as much precipitation every year as the low-lying land along the Rio Grande (thirty-five inches a year, on average, versus twelve). And although lower elevations are generally warmer and have longer growing seasons, at night cold air drains down from the high mountains and makes valley bottoms much colder and their frost-free seasons shorter than those of many mid-elevation zones. These patterns of cold air drainage affected ancestral Puebloans' decisions about where to live and farm.

Precipitation is particularly capricious in the Jemez Mountain region, creating additional challenges for prehistoric farmers. Predictably, the higher the elevation, the more snow falls in winter, but summer thunderstorms are much more erratic in where they unburden themselves. In the lower Pajarito Plateau farmlands away from the moun-

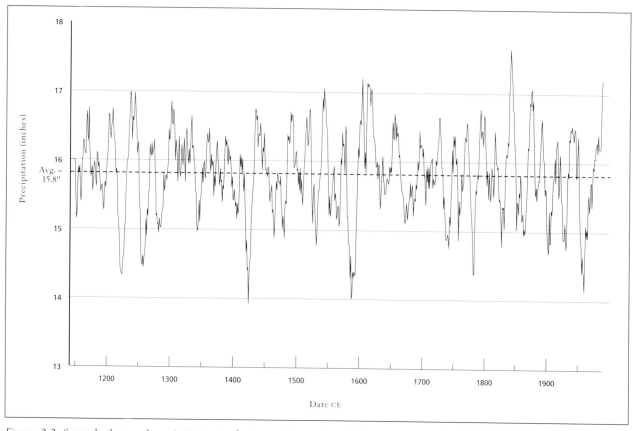

Figure 2.2. Smoothed annual precipitation in the Jemez Mountains, 1150–1990 CE, as reconstructed from tree rings.

tains, rainfall is especially irregular. (Chapter 4 describes how farmers handled this unpredictable climate.)

Even more importantly, rain and snow in the Southwest are highly uneven from year to year, driven by faraway changes in ocean temperatures and the position of the jet stream. Weather records for the last eighty years show that although total yearly rainfall and snowfall at Bandelier National Monument headquarters averaged about sixteen inches, measurements ranged from as little as five inches to as much as twenty-six inches a year. These records reveal severe, multiyear droughts in the 1930s and 1950s and another beginning in the late 1990s, with serious effects on the agricultural economy of New Mexico.

Tree-ring reconstructions of climate, which stretch back more than two thousand years for the Southwest, show that extreme variability in precipitation has existed for at least that long. Ancestral Puebloans endured many severe droughts, some decades long. For example, tree rings record

extreme multiyear droughts in the Jemez Mountains in the 1220s, 1250s, and 1280s, around 1340, and in the 1420s and 1580s. Many shorter wet and dry spells came and went throughout those centuries. Because plants in this unpredictable, semiarid climate begin to experience water stress when the weather is dry for even a few weeks, early farmers clearly had to use ingenuity and local knowledge to make a living.

Surface water has always been scarce in this landscape. Evaporation exceeds annual precipitation, and volcanic soils and bedrock absorb much storm runoff. Across the entire Pajarito Plateau, only Santa Clara Creek and Frijoles Creek usually flow year-round all the way to the Rio Grande. The amount of water in streams and springs is closely tied to seasonal and annual precipitation, resulting in huge swings in the volume of surface water available over time. For example, in many drier years, the lowest portion of even Frijoles Creek stops flowing. Although springs emerge at the base of the higher mountains and near the Rio Grande, few

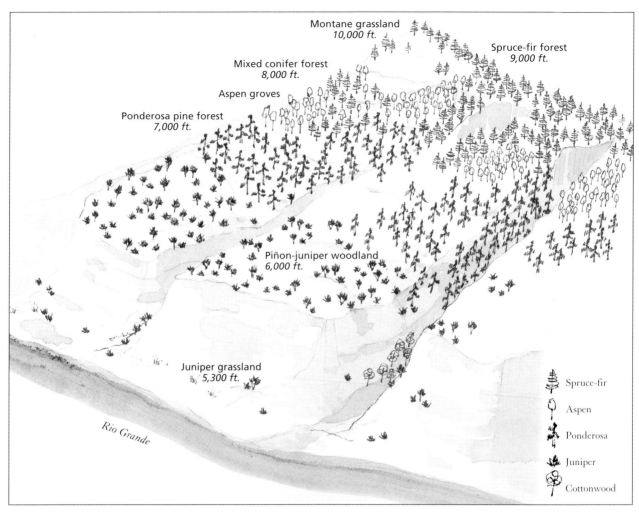

Montane grassland
10,000 ft.

Spruce-fir forest
9,000 ft.

Mixed conifer forest
8,000 ft.

Aspen groves

Ponderosa pine forest
7,000 ft.

Piñon-juniper woodland
6,000 ft.

Juniper grassland
5,300 ft.

Rio Grande

Spruce-fir

Aspen

Ponderosa

Juniper

Cottonwood

Figure 2.3. Plant communities and their elevations in the Pajarito landscape.

exist today in the heart of the Pajarito Plateau, perhaps partly because denser forests over the past one hundred years have reduced spring and stream flows.

The scarcity of water for domestic—that is, nonagricultural—uses must have posed an enormous challenge for prehistoric Puebloans, especially during droughts. How did thousands of Pajaritans, living mostly on the dry mesa tops, get enough water for their daily needs for more than three hundred years? They likely hauled a lot of water up from adjoining canyon streams—perhaps this was a job for children. Rainwater collects in rocky hollows in drainage bottoms, and ancestral Puebloans surely made good use of such natural pools of storm runoff. They probably also collected rainwater that ran off cliff faces and the roofs of their dwellings, storing it in jars and ground-level reservoirs.

Archaeologists have found eight reservoirs on dry mesa tops around Bandelier's three largest village sites—Tsankawi, Yapashi, and San Miguel. Even winter water can be hard to come by, because stream flows are low and standing water freezes. Perhaps the Pajaritans used their most common pottery type, dark-colored jars, to collect and sunmelt snow for domestic use.

Vegetation Patterns and Fire

The flora of the Pajarito Plateau is quite diverse: more than 750 species of plants grow today in Bandelier National Monument. They form vegetation communities in distinctive zones related to elevation and slope exposure. From the warm, dry canyon slopes along the Rio Grande to the cooler, wetter peaks of the Jemez, juniper grasslands give way to mesa-top woodlands of piñon and juniper

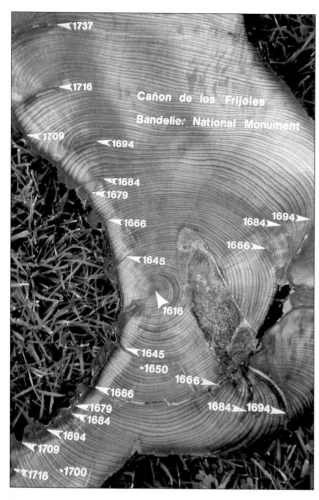

Figure 2.4. Cross section of a fire-scarred ponderosa pine, showing the calendar years of fires.

and then forests of ponderosa pine, mixed forests of Douglas fir, white fir, ponderosa pine, and aspen, and finally forests of Engelmann spruce and cork-bark fir on the cold north slopes of the highest peaks. Ancient montane grasslands grace upper south-facing summit slopes, and large, moist meadows blanket interior basins such as the Valle Grande.

Natural disturbances such as fires, floods, and droughts also affect plant life. Lightning-caused fires have been a principal force shaping the land-scape of the Jemez Mountains. Fire scars found in local tree rings show that surface fires once burned through Jemez forests every five to twenty-five years. Droughts brought fires that burned across the entire Frijoles Creek watershed every twenty years or so. Several times a century, most of the Jemez range burned in a single year, mostly in low-severity surface fires that charred grasses and pine needles. Severe droughts also cause trees and shrubs to die back and succumb to insect attacks. These natural disturbances restrain the buildup of thick forests and favor more diverse communities with abundant grasses, flowering herbs, and shrubs.

Animals

Many types of animals live in the habitats of the Pajarito Plateau. Among the fifty-six mammal species currently found in Bandelier National Monument are mule deer, cottontail rabbits, and elk. More than 110 bird species have been recorded nesting in the park, including game birds such as wild turkeys and blue grouse. Sandhill cranes and a variety of ducks and geese use the Rio Grande as an important migratory corridor. Native Americans also ate fish, and there are eighteen fish species in Bandelier today.

Through overhunting, predator control, and habitat alteration, people have caused many animal species of the Pajarito to become locally extinct. Missing species include human prey such as bighorn sheep, pronghorn antelope, prairie dogs, jackrabbits, and several Rio Grande fish species. Eels used to migrate to these headwaters from the Gulf of Mexico until they were blocked by dams. Other ecologically important extinctions are those of two top predators that competed with humans—grizzly bears and gray wolves. Historically, people also introduced foreign animal species into this landscape. Spanish colonists in the 1600s brought domestic sheep, cattle, horses, and burros. Feral burros and cattle roamed Bandelier until the 1990s, and a wild horse herd still lives just across the Rio Grande on the Caja del Rio Plateau west of Santa Fe.

Landscape Continuity and Change

Patterns of climate, vegetation, and fire have fol-lowed the same basic course for the past nine thou-sand years or so on the Pajarito Plateau, according to pollen and charcoal evidence from the central Jemez Mountains. Recurrent droughts and fires kept forests and woodlands relatively open, encour-aging productive understories of grass and other herbaceous plants. This grassy cover stabilized and

Figure 2.5. A surface fire in Bandelier National Monument, typical of low-severity natural fires.

Figure 2.6. An unnaturally dense forest in upper Frijoles Canyon, providing fuel for canopy fires.

human land-use practices over the past thousand years.

How did ancestral Puebloans change this landscape? Their effects on the Pajarito Plateau may have been relatively inconspicuous or circumscribed until the population boom of the late 1100s. From then until the mid-1500s, thousands of people called Bandelier home. These early farmers probably deforested the already open mesa tops as they cut trees to clear land for fields, build their homes, heat their living quarters in winter, and cook their meals. Ancestral Puebloans required about one acre of cultivated land to feed each person, and planting had to be rotated over time to allow the soil to recover its fertility. Thus thousands of acres must have been in use at any one time. Most of the mesa-top area in Bandelier was likely disturbed by shifting slash-and-burn agriculture over the course of these centuries. Although people felled trees with stone axes and fire girdling and used digging sticks and stone-tipped hoes to plant and weed their crops (they had no draft animals or plows), the cumulative effect of all this human action on the semiarid soils probably

enriched the plateau's soils for millennia. Yet despite the dynamic stability of this long-term pattern, the Bandelier landscape has been markedly altered by

was localized water and wind erosion.

Both farming and hunting took their toll on some animal populations. In the steep terrain of the Bandelier area, mule deer and bighorn sheep were important prey, as we see in the bones found during archaeological excavations of ancient houses. The near absence of elk bones in local archaeological sites may mean that Indian hunting had decimated nearby elk herds. The cleared mesa tops, however, would have favored species that needed open habitats, such as prairie dogs and jackrabbits, and the Puebloans ate them, too.

By the mid-1500s the Puebloan people had moved off the Pajarito Plateau, settling in adjoining river valleys. Perhaps four centuries' worth of depletion of wood, soil, and game animals contributed to this emigration. By the time of Spanish settlement in 1598, the Pajarito Plateau was largely uninhabited, and periodic incursions by raiding Navajos helped keep it that way until the mid- to late 1800s. Grassy vegetation quickly covered old fields, and soils stabilized. Trees established themselves more slowly in the face of frequent natural fires. Wildlife populations readjusted to habitat changes and reduced hunting pressures.

A Landscape of the Future

During a mere twenty-two years of studying the Jemez Mountains, I have witnessed some dramatic changes in the landscape. A severe drought and warm temperatures since 1996 have amplified the rate of change in vegetation on the Pajarito Plateau. Crown fires (see plate 24) have scorched tens of thousands of acres on and adjoining the plateau. Drought-stressed trees have been dying by the millions, many of them pushed over the edge by exploding populations of native bark beetles. Fires and die-back have effectively returned local forests to the lower, more naturally sustainable densities of earlier times. As the drought has deepened, forest dieback has extended upslope and begun to include Douglas firs. If forecasts of persistent regional drought prove correct, many more trees will soon begin to die even in the high forests of the Jemez Mountains. Local land managers are now mechanically thinning trees in large tracts to try to reduce the risk of further crown fires.

The possibility that accelerating global climate change is contributing to the magnitude and pace of these landscape transformations is worrisome,

Figure 2.7. Soil erosion in Bandelier, a product of human use and historic overgrazing. The exposed tree roots attest to severe soil loss.

yet a longer historical perspective reminds us that the Jemez Mountains have endured similar transitions in the discernable past. Time will tell whether this living land will sustain its resilience in the face of new human pressures.

Craig D. Allen is a research ecologist with the U.S. Geological Survey and leader of the Jemez Mountains Field Station at Bandelier National Monument.

Figure 3.1. Archaic-period mano and milling stone.

Ancient Foragers of the High Desert Country

Bradley J. Vierra

It has often been pointed out that for 99 percent of human history we lived our lives as hunter-gatherers. Our species, *Homo sapiens*, the most recent and successful hominid, evolved between two hundred thousand and fifty thousand years ago. Yet only in the last ten thousand years have we experimented with new ways of making a living.

In the American Southwest the transition from a hunting and gathering lifestyle took place even more recently—within the last thirty-five hundred years. Before that, people throughout the Southwest, including the Pajarito Plateau, lived in small, mobile family groups, moving in response to the seasonal availability of wild plants and animals. During their annual rounds they collected information about when and where to expect fruits and nuts to ripen, where to find good hunting grounds, and where to look for useful stone to refurbish their tool kits. Our forebears understood the ecology and habitats of all the potential food species they might seek. Being in the right place at the right time was critical to survival.

For millennia, hunter-gatherers lived in campsites. From them they walked as much as ten miles a day to stalk prey or gather plant foods. They used each campsite until they had depleted the resources nearby or until the seasons changed and food became available elsewhere. Modern hunter-gatherers in similar arid environments live in groups of about twenty people and can cover more than thirty-five hundred square miles in their annual quest for food. Although we often think of these foragers as living a harsh life and barely surviving from day to day,

that probably is not the case. Studies of the !Kung San of the Kalahari Desert in southern Africa show that they spend about twenty hours a week hunting and gathering—half our forty-hour work week.

There is in fact much to admire about the hunter-gatherer lifestyle. Ancient hunter-gatherers were not only physically fit but also enjoyed a diet that modern nutritionists would like the rest of us to emulate. More than anyone since, hunter-gatherers lived lightly on the landscape. They built rough shelters or occupied caves when the weather required it, but otherwise they lived outdoors and moved frequently. They were also masters of the terrain. They knew the location of every spring, plant, and animal in territories that often covered thousands of square miles. And they were ingenious and daring hunters who pursued big game with the simplest of weapons—weapons so finely crafted that only a few modern flint knappers have successfully duplicated them.

All of this helps to explain why archaeologists dedicate their careers to pursuing and understanding these elusive people, whose presence is often indicated by no more than a shattered stone tool or the remnants of an ancient hearth. What it does not explain is why our ancestors ever abandoned such an apparently free and simple life. Let me describe what researchers have learned about hunter-gatherers around the Pajarito Plateau and how their lifestyle gradually changed over several thousand years.

Hunter-gatherers were the first people to live on the Pajarito Plateau and in the adjacent valleys. They inhabited the region for 10,000 of the 11,500

Figure 3.2. How to use an atlatl.

years during which people have been present there. Living in small groups, they moved seasonally between uplands and lowlands, hunting animals, especially bison in the lower grasslands, and foraging for wild plants. From river valley to mountaintop, the land offered plentiful resources, including a glassy obsidian that made the sharpest of cutting tools.

Today, little evidence of these Paleoindian and Archaic foragers survives. Archaeologists have discovered only isolated dart points of their making and a few ancient campsites with hearths, milling stones, and flakes. The challenge is to understand the past from these few remains: what foods the people collected or hunted, during which seasons of the year they lived on the plateau, and where they came from and moved to.

The Paleoindian Period (9500–6000 BCE)

It was archaeological finds in New Mexico that first proved the antiquity of humans in North America. In the early 1900s, bones of extinct animals were uncovered together with spear or dart points at ancient campsites near the towns of Folsom and Clovis in eastern New Mexico. The early hunter-gatherers who camped there, and others of their era, are called Paleoindians, and they lived during a time of transition from the last ice age to modern climatic conditions spanning the millennia from about 9500 to 6000 BCE. Isolated spear points unique to the Paleoindian period are often the only traces left of these first inhabitants.

The earlier of two types of spear points, the Clovis point, defines the earlier of two Paleoindian subperiods, the Clovis period. Archaeological finds dating to this period, between 9500 and 8900 BCE, give us the earliest firm evidence of inhabitants of the New World. Clovis hunters used distinctive "lanceolate" dart points, tapered like the head of a lance. Clovis points have been discovered in the Rio Grande Valley near Albuquerque and Santa Fe and in uplands of New Mexico including the Pajarito Plateau, Polvadera Mesa, and the Sangre de Cristo Mountains. In northern New Mexico these spear points are quite large—three to four inches long. They have a distinctive "flute," or scar, running from the base of the point toward its tip. This flute was used to fasten the dart point tightly to a fore-shaft, which was then fixed to a spear.

The hunter threw the spear not by hand but by using an atlatl—a throwing stick that enabled the hunter to throw the spear farther and more accurately. An atlatl is about two feet long and two inches wide. The hunter places the feathered butt of the spear in a notch at the end of the stick, and his fingers fit into two loops at the front of the stick. The atlatl increased the length of the hunter's arm by an additional two feet, allowing him to throw the six-foot-long spear up to forty yards. This technology worked well for hunting large game in open fields. The foreshaft could also be detached from the spear and the point used as a large knife to butcher the animal.

Because ancient ground surfaces are continually

being eroded or buried, archaeologists in New Mexico have found only a few isolated Clovis points left by ancient hunters (see plate 3). Two points came from the Pajarito Plateau, both made of white chalcedony, which is conducive to producing large flaked implements. Thick layers of chalcedony and chert outcrop at Cerro Pedernal near Abiquiu, New Mexico. A third Clovis point, found near Santa Fe, is made of a reddish stone with dark red lines, a material that is not found locally but could be from either Texas or Colorado. This is important: the distance between the place where the raw material was quarried and the place where spear point was discarded is a clue to the size of the area traveled by Clovis people.

No Clovis campsites have been found on the Pajarito Plateau, but isolated camps with evidence of stone tool making have been identified up and down the Rio Grande Valley. One of the most fascinating of these is the Zapata Mammoth site in the San Luis Valley near Great Sand Dunes National Park and Preserve, Colorado. It is one of several sites in the American Southwest with mammoth remains and Clovis points. We cannot be sure, however, how much Clovis hunters relied on mammoths. The huge skeletons of these elephant-size animals (see plate 4) survive well and are dramatically visible. Because of the excellent preservation of mammoth bones, the spear points used to kill the animals can be found in their original relationship to the bones. The bones of smaller game animals are much more likely to decompose over the millennia, leaving little for archaeologists to unearth except an occasional solitary point.

We know somewhat more about the slightly later Folsom period (8900 to 8000 BCE), again named after its characteristic spear point, than we do about the Clovis period. Archaeological evidence of the Folsom period is more common in the Rio Grande Valley than on the Pajarito Plateau, where only two Folsom points have been found. Unlike Clovis points, which appear all across North America, Folsom points are limited to the Rio Grande Valley, adjacent parts of the Rocky Mountains, and the Great Plains, where bison hunting was an important activity. During this period, rainfall increased, and richer grasslands supported larger bison herds.

Near Albuquerque, archaeologists usually find Folsom sites around dry lake beds known as playas. In earlier, wetter times, playas were filled with water, and a hunter could count on finding herds of thirsty bison at them. Some sites were lookouts, situated so that hunters had a good view of the terrain and could make or mend hunting gear while watching for game. Others were kill sites, located right next to playas, where hunters also butchered the meat and—judging from the presence of stone scrapers—cleaned the hides. Last, campsites lay between all these areas. The camps were probably where family groups lived, cooked their meals, tossed away broken tools, and made new ones.

Figure 3.3. Broken sections of Folsom points.

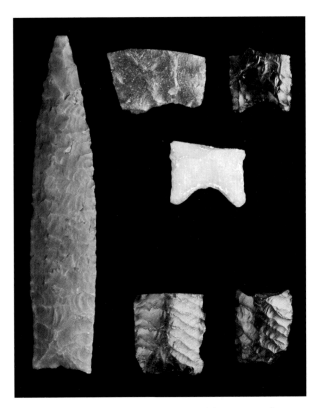

Figure 3.4. Late Paleoindian points and fragments of points.

Together these archaeological sites show us how Folsom life involved hunting small herds of bison that came to drink at the playas and ponds.

What was Folsom people's annual round? The sources of stone from which they made their tools give us an idea of how far they ranged. In the Albuquerque area, Folsom points were often made of stone obtained from gravels along the Rio Grande, but a few tools consist of stone from distant quarries. Judging from the known sources of the exotic stone, Folsom groups moved seasonally between the central Rio Grande Valley, the San Juan Basin in the west, and the Jemez Mountains and upper Rio Grande Valley near Chama to the north. Perhaps Folsom people hunted and gathered in the mountains in late summer, moved into the valley for bison hunting in the fall, and stayed there over the winter. If so, they might have hunted and gathered on the Pajarito Plateau during the mid- to late summer.

The Late Paleoindian period (8000 to 6000 BCE) was, in comparison with the Folsom period, warmer and drier. Playas evaporated in the Albuquerque

area, and game moved to perennial streams. Late Paleoindian people appear to have followed the game, setting up camps along streams. We find Late Paleoindian spear points in both upland and lowland settings, suggesting that Paleoindians at this time were still hunting bison in the Rio Grande Valley and exploiting plants and animals on the Pajarito Plateau.

Four isolated points represent this time period on the Pajarito. Two of them are made of obsidian from the Jemez Mountains, and two are formed of an orthoquartzite that outcrops near Abiquiu. Unlike Clovis and Folsom points, Late Paleoindian points have no flutes. They are either short, wide points with concave bases or long, narrow points with square bases. The former type has been found on the Pajarito Plateau, and the latter, at a site on the Caja del Rio Plateau.

The Archaic Period (6000 BCE–500 CE)
Archaeologists do not fully understand the transition from the Paleoindian to the Archaic lifestyle in what is now northern New Mexico. It involved a shift in people's seasonal movements from following abundant game animals to following the availability of plants at different times and places. Because this change was so dramatic, archaeologists have wondered whether Late Paleoindian people of the region were even the ancestors of the later Archaic people.

One explanation is that as the climate grew drier, bison herds retreated to the Great Plains, and Late Paleoindian hunters followed them. The abandoned Rio Grande Valley was then taken over by different people, hunter-gatherers from the west who already relied on a variety of plants and animals and used what we define as Early Archaic dart points, similar to those found in southern California and Arizona.

An alternative and more likely explanation is that the same people lived there all along but simply adapted to changing local conditions. Plants and small game became more important during the Late Paleoindian era and continued to be so in the Early Archaic. Perhaps hunter-gatherers began to rely more heavily on a diet of seasonal plants during the centuries when piñon-juniper woodlands were replacing grasslands. As fall hunts in the Rio

Figure 3.5. Archaic-period dart points.

Grande Valley became less successful, people shifted their residences to the uplands to collect piñon nuts and hunt deer. Rather than drying bison meat, they stored piñon nuts, an important source of protein, for the winter months.

Archaic sites on the Pajarito Plateau are camps represented by isolated hearths and the debris of obsidian tool manufacturing. They contain manos (hand stones) and milling stones for grinding wild seeds, as well as stone knives for butchering animals. The number of known sites on the plateau doubled during the Middle Archaic (4000–2000 BCE) and tripled during the Late Archaic (2000 BCE–500 CE). But this pattern may, like the survival of Clovis points and mammoth bones, be a result of geology and selective preservation. Early and Middle Archaic sites are often deeply buried in canyon bottoms and eroded away on mesa tops, so their smaller numbers might mean simply that

many sites have been destroyed or are not visible. Ancient campsites that are visible generally lie high in the ponderosa pine forest, indicating that people lived in them during a time of warmer and drier climate.

Archaic dart points differ from Paleoindian points. Each one has a blade, or cutting edge, that is distinct from the stem, or hafted base. In contrast, a Paleoindian point generally has no stem but instead a continuous edge from tip to base. These differences presumably reflect changes in the types of game Paleoindian and Archaic people hunted, the hunting techniques they used, and the general functions of the tools. Paleoindians might have used points as both darts and hafted knives. Early and Middle Archaic spear points on the Pajarito Plateau are made of Jemez Mountain obsidian and of basalt from the plateau and the Rio Grande Valley.

We find Late Archaic sites on the Pajarito

Figure 3.6. Maize from the Pajarito Plateau. The large ear at the back is recent. The ear at front left dates to 1200 BCE; the eight-row ear in the center and the twelve-row ear on the right are Puebloan and date to 1200–1400 CE.

Plateau in both juniper-savanna grasslands and mixed ponderosa pine and conifer forests at higher elevations. Judging from the seasonal abundances of seeds, nuts, and fruits in the area, I believe Late Archaic groups lived in the low grasslands during the early summer, when Indian rice grass seeds ripened. In the mid- to late summer they moved up into the ponderosa-conifer forest to harvest goosefoot, pigweed, wild onions, berries, and wild potatoes (see chapter 5). Hunters procured obsidian at nearby quarries at the same time. In the fall, families moved back down to the piñon-juniper woodlands to collect pine nuts, acorns, and yucca and cacti fruits. Their final destination for the year was the Rio Grande Valley, where they established winter camps. Archaic people probably hunted pronghorn in the valleys, deer in the mountains, and rabbits everywhere. They used manos and milling stones to process seeds and plants, and obsidian dart points to hunt game.

During the Late Archaic, some hunter-gatherers began to experiment with domesticated plants. Evidence from Jemez Cave, some twenty miles southwest of Frijoles Canyon, may help us understand this experimentation. There, archaeologists found maize dating to 1200 BCE. The residents of this site probably grew maize plants in the mudflats adjacent to a small lake. Their neighbors probably planted early maize in similar well-watered settings near piñon-juniper woodlands in other parts of the Rio Grande Valley, if not on the Pajarito Plateau. When families returned to the woodlands in October to collect nuts and fruits, they also harvested the corn. The plants were left to grow untended during the summer in order not to disrupt the existing seasonal routine. In the beginning, maize served merely as a backup when gathered foods fell short. This early variety of maize had a cob only two inches long—tiny in comparison with ancestral Pueblo maize, let alone modern corncobs. It certainly did not form the mainstay of the Late Archaic diet.

The big question is why, after thousands of years of hunting and gathering, these ancient people decided not only to include maize in their diet but also to grow it. The answer eludes us; several environmental and cultural factors probably came into play. From Clovis to Late Archaic times we see increasing evidence of change. Hunting territories shrank, partly because of population growth, until no single foraging group could roam the whole area. As the number of hunters rose, it became harder to find migratory game and therefore essential to depend more on plants. Eventually, wetter times during the Late Archaic made it possible to plant maize, and corn became a more reliable supplement to wild harvests. The use of maize spelled the beginning of the end of the ancient hunter-gatherer lifestyle in the high desert country. It also marked the beginning of the agricultural society of the ancestral Pueblo people, which we will see take off, much later, in Bandelier.

Bradley J. Vierra is a Paleoindian and Archaic specialist and an archaeologist with the Cultural Resources Team at Los Alamos National Laboratory.

Figure 4.1. Ancestral Pueblo farming terraces on a canyon slope.

Why Would Anyone Want to Farm Here?

Rory Gauthier and Cynthia Herhahn

Part of our job as archaeologists at Bandelier National Monument is to search for archaeological sites. It is wonderful, hot, dirty work. We spend the summer sleeping in tents, walk countless miles, scramble in and out of canyons, clamber over boulders, and struggle through thickets of trees and brush in our seemingly endless quest. On an average day we are rewarded with the discovery of six to ten new archaeological sites. Nearly half of them are field houses—simple stone-walled structures of one or two small rooms, now collapsed. Five hundred years ago these humble field houses sheltered farm families who tended nearby fields. Invariably, one of our less-seasoned crew members asks, "Why would anyone want to farm here?"

It's a good question. The mesa and canyon country encompassing Bandelier and the Pajarito Plateau is a beautiful, rugged, rocky landscape, but it is hard to imagine a less promising place to make a living as a farmer. Temperatures and the length of the growing season (the days between the last spring frost and the first fall frost) vary from year to year and can make or break a successful harvest. Frosts have been recorded in all months except July and August. Water, one of the most critical ingredients for successful agriculture, is just as scarce in Bandelier as it is in the rest of the arid Southwest. Bandelier and the Pajarito Plateau receive an average yearly precipitation—both rain and snow—of only sixteen inches, and slightly less than half of that falls during the summer growing season.

As if this weren't enough, droughts on the Pajarito are a sure bet. Archaeologists reconstruct climates in the Southwest by examining tree rings, and they have discovered that amounts of moisture falling as rain and snow varied tremendously on the plateau throughout the entire Puebloan occupation. Severe droughts struck between 1250 and 1290 CE and again between 1570 and 1597. The latter drought, which might have been one reason the Puebloans abandoned the plateau, was preceded by decades of dry weather spanning much of the 1500s.

What is more, we find evidence that the people farmed their fields for only short periods of time, suggesting that agriculture rapidly depleted the soil nutrients. Because of the susceptibility of plateau soils to erosion, Puebloan farmers may also have struggled with severe soil loss.

Yet despite these problems, Puebloans did farm here, and for much of the time between 1150 and 1600 they were successful, growing corn, beans, and squash even though the environmental deck seemed stacked against them. Today, as we walk across this rugged landscape, we are always amazed at the sheer number of settlements we find. The density of sites is a testament to Pueblo agricultural talents and tenacity over a span of nearly four hundred years. "How did they do it?" we ask ourselves when we come across yet another field house. They did it by using ingenious farming techniques, though ultimately even Puebloan ingenuity may have failed to surmount long droughts and loss of soil fertility.

Puebloan Farming Strategies in the Bandelier Area

The northern Rio Grande Valley is known for the diversity of farming techniques its Puebloan farmers used. The mesas and canyons of the Pajarito Plateau slope gently to the southeast from the Jemez Mountains to the Rio Grande. The area that the Pueblo people used most heavily for agriculture lies between 5,300 and 7,300 feet above sea level. Snowfall and rainfall vary here from about eighteen inches a year at higher elevations to some twelve inches lower down. But higher elevations have cooler temperatures and shorter growing seasons than do lower elevations. These differences in climate within short distances on the Pajarito make diversification one of the most effective agricultural strategies. Ancestral Pueblo farmers diversified by using many different farming techniques and by planting fields in different settings.

Evidence of farming techniques lies everywhere on the Pajarito. We find the remains of Puebloans' efforts to conserve soil moisture, harvest snow and rainwater, and bring streamwater to fields. They built contour terraces and check dams—low alignments of rocks laid perpendicular to a slope or natural drainage—to slow runoff. They planted in "grid" gardens bordered by rows of rocks in order to slow erosion and retain moisture. They mulched some gardens with gravel or even piles of cobbles for the same reasons and to protect plants from early killing frosts. These modifications worked in winter as well, trapping blowing snow in much the way a drift fence along a highway does, enhancing soil moisture in the spring.

Farmers hedged their bets by planting fields in many different environmental settings. By establishing fields at higher elevations, they ensured that their crops would receive more rainfall, though they risked a killing frost. By planting at a lower elevation as well, they increased the odds of an ample growing season, though their crops might do poorly if too little rain fell. And planting fields at several elevations meant that if one field were destroyed by insects or rabbits and another failed because of drought, a third might still produce a good crop.

One result of our survey work is that we are able to see exactly how farmers shifted the locations of their pueblos and fields. From approximately 1150 to 1250 CE they moved their settlements from middle to higher elevations, presumably to take advantage of greater rain and snowfall. But they also ventured into some new zones at lower elevations in order to spread their risk. Between 1250 and 1290, a time of serious drought, they withdrew to the high places, in some cases going as far up as 7,400 feet.

Throughout the entire span of the Coalition Period, from 1150 to 1325—whatever the climate—farmers on the Pajarito were highly mobile, living in most of their pueblos for a generation or less. When we excavate these sites, we find little household rubbish or evidence of remodeling, sure signs of short occupancy. What is more, roof beams and building stones are often missing, suggesting that people took them away to reuse them in a new pueblo. We cannot tell whether the farmers left their pueblos in order to move to wetter or warmer spots or whether they had to move because their crops did poorly in depleted soils; this is a matter of debate.

By 1325 farmers had begun to abandon their hamlets and build a few larger pueblos instead. They lived in these villages—including the ones we know as Yapashi, San Miguel, Shohakka Pueblo, and Tyuonyi in Bandelier National Monument and Tshirege, Tsankawi, Otowi, and Puye on the northern Pajarito Plateau—over the next one hundred to two hundred years. Now, instead of moving their homes when fields wore out or rain stopped falling, they simply moved the field houses where they spent the summers. During much of the Classic period, farmers living in large pueblos constructed hundreds of field houses. They still maintained multiple fields and planted mostly on mesa tops, but they also began to use canyon bottoms where water running off steep canyon sides could be directed onto fields.

Farming Techniques

Among the Pajarito farmers' many practices, the most common was to set fields on the gently sloping mesa tops where crops relied directly on precipitation. People wanted soils that could quickly absorb and retain rainfall, so they prized patches of

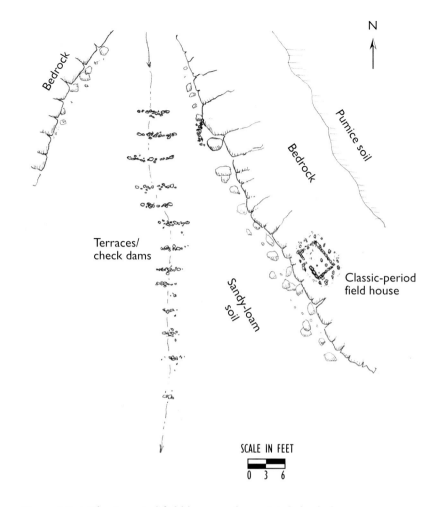

Figure 4.2. A Classic-period field house and associated check dams.

This loose, whitish gravel offered Puebloan farmers a choice environment during both the Coalition and Classic periods. Geologists describe the Pajarito pumice—fallout from the El Cajete volcanic eruptions approximately fifty-five thousand years ago—as a "Plinian" deposit, similar to that which buried the Roman city of Pompeii. The volcano ejected an estimated one cubic mile of pumice across the southern Jemez Mountains and the south-central portion of Bandelier National Monument. Carried by prevailing winds out of the southwest, the gravels drifted to the lee sides of canyons and ridges. Today, most of the pumice soil has been removed by erosion, but some relatively large deposits are still found in the south-central part of the monument near the prehistoric village of Yapashi. Pumice gravel patches can be as large as several hundred acres or as small as a scant acre, but even the smallest pumice slopes often have an associated field house.

For farmers, the important quality of pumice soils was their ability to absorb and hold moisture. Pumice is very coarse and porous, and in Bandelier it occurs as small pebbles. These absorb water quickly (somewhat like the vermiculite in modern potting soils) and then allow it to soak into the underlying layer, a mixture of pumice, silt, and clay into which plants send their roots. The ability of pumice soils to retain moisture from winter snowfall was particularly important to Puebloan farmers in the frequently dry late spring and early summer, when germinating seeds and young plants needed moisture.

In addition, pumice gravel, once penetrated by water, acts as a mulch, insulating the underlying soil against evaporation. It also keeps the deeper

volcanic pumice underlain by finer, clayey soil. For fields in drainages and canyons, they often constructed contour terraces and check dams in order to trap soil as well as the runoff after rainstorms. In a few places with permanent streams or springs, groups of farmers cooperated in building ditch systems to carry water to their fields. For most of the Puebloan history of the plateau, fields were situated on mesa tops and relied solely on rainfall, but as population grew and older fields began to require fallowing, farmers had to think up new techniques in order to cope.

Pumice Fields

Several years ago we began to recognize a connection between the presence of a field house and a type of soil unique to the Bandelier area: pumice.

Figure 4.3. North-facing pumice slope covered with snow.

soil cooler, because the rocky surface of the pumice reflects heat—something we know well from the hot days we have spent walking across it on survey. Many patches of pumice soil on the Pajarito, however, lie along cooler, northern exposures. This combination of qualities—water retention, insulation of the ground, and cool locations—appears to have made pumice soils ideal for Pueblo farmers. Typically, the soil is not compacted and is easy to work with a digging stick. Throughout most of the Puebloan era in Bandelier, people seem to have settled near these soils; few pumice patches lack a pueblo or field house.

Although they played a key role in farming on the Pajarito Plateau, pumice soils have one big drawback. They can lose their nutrients quickly, and they probably had to be left fallow for years before they could produce crops again. This was a problem common to mesa-top soils, too, because they so rarely received the infusions of organic matter

carried in runoff. Early in the agricultural history of Bandelier, people had many pristine pumice slopes to choose from. As population grew, prime fields became harder and harder to find. Once again farmers had to seek out new soils and develop new methods.

Recycling Pueblos

One of the Puebloans' most ingenious solutions to the problem of declining soil fertility was to turn abandoned pueblos into fields. Perhaps understandably, archaeologists were slow to recognize this technique. But Charlie Steen, a savvy, old-fashioned field archaeologist working on the northern Pajarito, found himself puzzled by odd stone alignments on the surfaces of collapsed pueblos and nearby refuse heaps. The alignments seemed strange because they appeared not to be walls. Steen excavated several of the pueblos and found that the stone alignments had been placed on the collapsed mounds after the

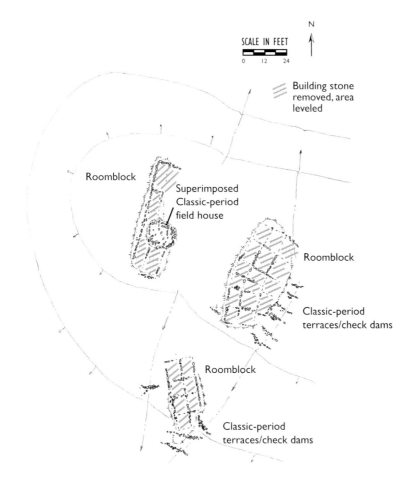

SCALE IN FEET

0 12 24

N

Building stone
removed, area
leveled

Roomblock

Superimposed
Classic-period
field house

Roomblock

Classic-period
terraces/check dams

Roomblock

Classic-period
terraces/check dams

Figure 4.4. Coalition-period roomblocks reused as fields in the Classic period.

helped trap runoff. In many cases, people had cleared and leveled the top of the rubble mound and used the stubs of the original walls as garden borders. Not only did we find terraces and borders, but we could also see the remains of small field houses super-imposed on the house mounds, built of stone recycled from the original structure.

When we compare the pottery of the original pueblo with pottery from the later agricultural features, it looks as if 50 to 150 years passed before Classic-period Puebloans planted fields on the ruined villages. The timing of this reuse is significant. During the Classic period, farmers put up field houses near every possible patch of arable land. These were simple con-structions, used only as temporary residences during the growing season, so they could be easily abandoned when the nearby fields were fallowed. This proliferation of field houses dur-ing the Classic period suggests that farmers were moving their fields increasingly often, desperately seeking good soil as fertility waned after years of farming. One can imagine that the rich soils contained with-in the walls of former pueblos made these choice agricultural spots.

Classic-Period Irrigation Systems

Even though Pueblo farmers established fields in every fertile spot on the Pajarito Plateau and regu-larly fallowed their farmsites, they struggled end-lessly to find enough good agricultural land and to contend with the vagaries of yearly precipitation. In Bandelier and one or two other locations on the plateau, a few permanent water sources gave peo-ple the opportunity to irrigate fields with con-structed ditch systems rather than having to wait for rain. As the climate grew drier in the late 1400s and 1500s, farmers developed irrigation systems in these places.

Adolph Bandelier is the first person known to

structures were abandoned and reduced to debris. He gradually realized that these features were stone borders, terraces, and check dams for garden plots. He reasoned that the Puebloans had used old house mounds as fields in order to take advantage of soil nutrients contained in the decomposing garbage, feces, and other organic matter left there by past inhabitants. Steen, ever ready with a pithy phrase, called this "passive manuring."

In Bandelier National Monument, similar stone alignments on the surfaces of Coalition-period pueblos form agricultural terraces and garden bor-ders. Crowning the tops of some of these house mounds are the remains of one- and two-room field houses. We carefully examined these pueblos-turned-fields and discovered that all the loose building stone had been taken off the rubble mound and placed on the sides of the mound to form the terraces, which reduced soil erosion and

Figure 4.5. A stone-lined irrigation ditch built by ancestral Pueblo farmers.

have described in writing, in his daily journal, the remains of an ancient *acequia*, or ditch, in Frijoles Canyon. Unfortunately, the location of Bandelier's acequia is unknown today, although it may survive as part of an irrigation ditch built by Judge A. J. Abbott, an early-twentieth-century homesteader who established a garden and orchard next to Tyuonyi Pueblo (see fig. 13.1). The Abbott ditch is approximately three-quarters of a mile long and capable of watering about thirty acres. Photographs taken before 1930 show that the entire area from Tyuonyi to the current National Park Service visitor's center was irrigated. Considering that nearly eight hundred Puebloans lived in Frijoles Canyon around 1500, we think the original ditch system must have watered more than the thirty acres farmed by Abbott.

Apart from Frijoles Canyon, few places in Bandelier National Monument offered farmers the option of irrigating their fields. Turkey Springs and small sections of Capulin Canyon have permanent streams and enough land suitable for farming, but altogether only about one hundred acres in the monument could have been farmed using irrigation methods.

North of Bandelier lie additional permanent or semipermanent sources of water for irrigation. In one fascinating example of a prehistoric irrigation system, the Pajarito Springs site in White Rock Canyon, Puebloans diverted water from a spring through a series of stone-lined ditches to agricultural fields. This system is a marvel of engineering. The farmers built a main, or mother, ditch over half a mile long to divert and carry water to many

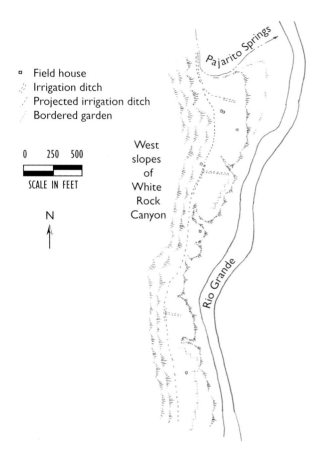

- Field house
- Irrigation ditch
- Projected irrigation ditch
- Bordered garden

0   250   500

SCALE IN FEET

N

West
slopes
of
White
Rock
Canyon

Pajarito Springs

Rio Grande

Figure 4.6. A prehistoric irrigation system in White Rock Canyon.

separate plots. The ditch traversed rugged slopes along the edge of White Rock Canyon, crossed a gradient of elevations, and supplied water to sixty acres of farmland. The fields watered by this system included gravel-mulch plots, bordered gardens, and grid gardens. It is clear from this careful landscaping that even with reliable water from irrigation, the Puebloans recognized the need to conserve soil moisture.

Elsewhere on the northern plateau, old maps show an irrigation ditch near the Classic-period village of Puye. Permanent streams once flowed through the canyons near the pueblos of Tshirege, Tsankawi, and Otowi. Archaeologists have not identified any ditch systems in these canyons, but perhaps they have not looked hard enough.

Although we still know little about irrigation on the Pajarito Plateau, it seems to have been a minor agricultural strategy. Despite the potential productivity of the canyon bottoms, they contain only small patches of irrigable land in comparison with the ample mesa tops. As a result, the mesas were clearly the Puebloans' first choice in farmland.

Epilogue

Mesa-top dry farming formed the backbone of Puebloan agriculture on the Pajarito Plateau. When farmers could no longer depend on this strategy, they found their options limited. After successfully farming one of the Southwest's more challenging landscapes for more than four hundred years, the people of the plateau, now suffering from the gradual loss of nutrients in the soil together with one of the worst droughts in the history of the Southwest, could barely survive. They were early victims of the Southwest's fragile environment and unpredictable boom-and-bust climatic cycles.

A new chapter in this saga began in the late 1890s, when agricultural fields on the Pajarito, abandoned for over three hundred years, were once again made productive. Spanish and Anglo-American homesteaders, taking advantage of a stretch of good weather, began to farm pinto beans there commercially. For their own use they raised corn, squash, peas, and pumpkins. Their ambitious efforts were rewarded at first, but in the 1930s dry conditions returned, and some farmers resorted to hauling water from the Rio Grande by wagon. Others sensibly gave up farming altogether to pursue other livelihoods. Within a single forty-year interval the homesteaders unknowingly played out a scenario seen many times before on the Pajarito Plateau.

Rory Gauthier was a member of the Bandelier Archaeological Survey and is the park archaeologist at Bandelier National Monument. Cynthia Herhahn is a doctoral candidate at the University of California at Santa Barbara and an archaeologist at Bandelier National Monument.

Figure 5.1. Wild turkeys in New Mexico.

Rabbits, Turkeys, and Maize

five

Kari M. Schmidt and Meredith H. Matthews

We often take friends and family who are visiting the high desert for the first time to see the countless archaeological sites scattered across the Pajarito Plateau. One question is never far from their minds: What did the Pajaritans eat? In our modern world, getting meals means a trip to the grocery store or a call to the local pizza place. The variety of food available to us is astounding. We can hardly imagine hunting, gathering, and farming to obtain everything we need. But that is exactly what the early people of the Pajarito Plateau did every day, year-round, in order to make a living. Although the plateau and the adjacent Rio Grande Valley abounded in plant and animal resources, daily life for inhabitants of the high desert was still an uncertain, often risky business. Nowhere were the uncertainties felt more pointedly than in the Pajaritans' quest for food.

What, then, did they eat? How and what did they hunt? How did they prepare their meat? How did they gather wild plants, and what did they do to make them edible? Some of these questions we can address directly through archaeological and ethnographic research; others we can only speculate about. The archaeological record provides evidence of some of the Pajaritans' "groceries" in the remains of what they hunted, gathered, and cultivated. With this evidence, and taking into consideration the cultural as well as the environmental circumstances of Pajaritan life, we explore how and why these groceries changed through time.

Reconstructing Ancient Cuisine

Archaeologists find the best and most direct evidence of what prehistoric people ate in the remains of animals and plants preserved in ancient habitations, hearths, and garbage heaps. We also find clues to diet in human skeletal remains, coprolites (desiccated feces), pollen, and artifacts such as stone tools and pottery vessels. In particular, zooarchaeology, the study of human use of animals in the past, and paleoethnobotany, the study of past human use of plants, help us learn what people ate.

We have collected plant and animal remains from sites spanning more than two thousand years on the Pajarito Plateau. These items give us only a partial record of what constituted the prehistoric diet. Because food remains are fragile, the evidence is often skewed by what is preserved. Even soil composition affects our clues: the volcanic pumice–based soil of the Pajarito, for example, is rough on delicate fibers, seeds, and bones. And of course the very act of eating removes evidence of many plants

Figure 5.2. Dried beans and squash parts.

from the archaeological record. This is one reason corn appears in archaeological sites far more often than squash and beans. Corncobs are inedible, and we find them in abundance, whereas beans and squash are eaten whole, and nothing is left to find.

We also use ethnographic information—interviews, notes, and publications—about historic-period and contemporary Pueblo people to gain insights into diet, food preferences, and food preparation that might apply to the past. Such information is especially relevant for understanding prehistoric diet on the Pajarito Plateau, because the people of the modern Tewa pueblos of Santa Clara, San Juan, and San Ildefonso and the Keresan pueblo of Cochiti are descendents of the Pajaritans. We know from historic accounts how Pueblo people ground dried corn on metates (mealing stones), cured meat, dried animal hides on racks, and gathered piñon nuts, chokecherries, and goosefoot seeds in baskets and clay bowls, and how they prepared them.

Paleoindian and Archaic Foods

Although we don't know how heavily Southwestern Paleoindian hunters relied on mammoths and other large mammals, it is clear that they successfully hunted these formidable creatures (see chapter 3). Nonetheless, with the extinction of such prey at the end of the last ice age, Paleoindian and later Archaic people gradually turned to smaller game and wild plants.

The Pajaritan diet during the Late Archaic period (2000 BCE–500 CE) is a good example of the results of this shift. Plants used primarily as sources of food during those centuries included hackberry, juniper, oak, prickly pear, piñon pine, pigweed (amaranth), goosefoot (chenopodium), yucca, squawberry, purslane, and sunflower. Animals used for food at Late Archaic sites included fish, duck, turkey, grouse, prairie dog, ground squirrel, jackrabbit, cottontail rabbit, beaver, gray fox, bobcat, mountain lion, bison, mountain sheep, mule deer, and pronghorn.

Figure 5.3. Deer in Bandelier National Monument.

Rabbits, used for both their meat and their fur, were a staple. Rabbit remains appear in nearly every archaeological site on the plateau. Many ethnographic accounts and oral histories of Southwestern tribes and pueblos describe how people procured rabbits: with bows and arrows, snares, and pitfall traps and by extracting them from their burrows with sticks. Some rabbits, usually jackrabbits, were even hunted communally in large drives for which whole villages turned out, using nets to corral the animals. During historic times, rabbit drives were documented for the Hopi people and for Zia, Sandia, and Santa Ana Pueblos.

Adolph Bandelier, in his journal of November 6, 1880, described preparations for a rabbit drive at Cochiti. Thirty years later, Elsie Clews Parsons recorded virtually identical details:

> In October 1913, I happened to be passing through Cochiti the day of a hunt, and at a distance I saw the start and the gay homecom-

ing. Riding into town about 9 am we passed about an eighth of a mile to the north-east of the town an elderly man sitting at prayer before a small fire. An hour or so later, in this locality, the hunters, men and women, gathered together and I heard singing. At sunset they returned. About an eighth of a mile to the northwest of the town, a group of men gathered together for a few minutes. The women in twos and threes came in on foot, laughing and talking and carrying the game—rabbits, small rodents, and quail. I was told that the woman first to reach a hunter after he has made a kill becomes the recipient.

Both Bandelier and Parsons commented on the rituals people performed in connection with rabbit drives—rituals perhaps signaling that such hunting dates back long before crops came to the Pajarito.

The Archaic way of life and its dietary patterns endured virtually uninterrupted until around 500 BCE, when Archaic people began to establish more permanent residences, although their use of the plateau was still mostly seasonal. Their adoption of a less mobile lifestyle may indicate that they were now planting and cultivating corn. Corn was grown at Jemez Cave as early as 1200 BCE. In other parts of the southern desert borderland, such as the Tucson Basin, people grew corn soon after its introduction from Mexico around 2000 BCE and, more significantly, relied heavily on it for food.

On the Pajarito Plateau, however, changes arising from the adoption of agriculture took hold more gradually. Not until long after their introduction from Mexico did domesticated crops become significant items in the Pajaritan grocery basket. Why did it take so long for corn to become important when it was such a reliable source of sustenance? Why did the Pajaritans continue to emphasize hunting and gathering when so many others around the Southwest were turning to agriculture? Good answers to these questions elude us, but part of the story may be simply that the Pajaritans didn't need to alter their way of life as early as some people elsewhere. The wild plants and animals of the plateau, combined with fairly low population densities during the Late Archaic, enabled them to continue to rely on their familiar, efficient hunting-and-gathering lifestyle. Later, as population increased, each group's territorial range shrank. At that point, agriculture became a more necessary means of making a living on the plateau.

Growing Corn and Raising Turkeys

When we compare the plants used during the Late Archaic with those of the Coalition period (1150–1325 CE), we find that the species are nearly identical. The relative proportions of the species change, however, and one singular difference arises: agriculture. During the Coalition years, Pajaritans began increasingly to practice dry farming—that is, farming dependent on rainfall rather than irrigation. Domesticated plant foods—corn, beans, and squash—became crucial parts of the diet. And the Pajaritans were successful farmers, so people enjoyed a fairly predictable food supply. Farmers also altered the natural landscape. As they cultivated more and more land, the areas where some wild food plants could grow shrank correspondingly.

Nevertheless, wild plants remained important food sources during the Coalition period. Excavations of Coalition sites show that people put assorted products on the menu besides corn, beans, and squash, many of them the same foods their Archaic predecessors had eaten: goosefoot, pigweed, sagebrush, piñon nuts, various grasses, wild legumes, purslane, chokecherry, squawbush, yucca, members of the rose family, and various cacti (see plate 7). Some of these plants, such as pigweed, goosefoot, and purslane, are called "pioneer" plants—they grow well in soil that has been disturbed by farming. They no doubt sprang up in Coalition-period fields, available for gathering. Pajaritans used many other

plants, too, whose remains we find on sites, probably for fuel, construction material, clothing, utensils, and medicines.

We find equally varied animal remains: catfish, prairie dog, ground squirrel, jackrabbit, cottontail rabbit, coyote, gray fox, bison, mountain sheep, mule deer, and pronghorn. Pajaritans used the bones and the hides or feathers of other animals and birds—porcupine, skunk, weasel, black bear, golden eagle, red-tailed hawk—to make tools, blankets, clothing, and anything else they needed for work and rituals.

Another domesticated item, the turkey, became a critical part of the Puebloan diet during the Coalition period, second in importance only to corn. Pajaritans had hunted and eaten wild turkeys for centuries, but during this period they began to raise them in pens in their villages.

At one Late Coalition site on the plateau, turkeys accounted for more than half the animal bones excavated, and two distinct sizes of mature turkey bones could be seen. Interestingly, the smaller bones were excavated from trash deposits, whereas the larger bones came from the kiva and the floors of two rooms. There are three possible explanations for this. First, people might have eaten wild turkeys and thrown their bones into the trash but used larger, domesticated turkeys, especially their feathers, in ceremonies, many of which took place in kivas. Second, the two sizes might have resulted simply from size differences between male and female turkeys ("sexual dimorphism"), with larger bones representing males (ceremonial use) and smaller bones representing females (being eaten). Third, the bones might represent two subspecies of turkeys, each used differently. Any of these scenarios means that Puebloans chose different sexes or types of turkeys for eating and for ritual use. What we know for certain is that the Pajaritans depended on a readily available food, the domesticated turkey, increasingly during the Coalition period.

Pajaritans sought food far and wide: they gathered plants in grasslands, along streams, in piñon-juniper and oak woodlands, and in coniferous forests. As a result, they enjoyed a wonderfully varied diet. The variety of foods not only contributed to good health but also helped balance the effects of crop failures. Nonetheless, because we find more

Figure 5.4. Charred corn found at Rainbow House in Frijoles Canyon.

maize and turkey remains in sites of the Coalition period than in earlier ones, it is clear that people by this time were putting considerable effort into raising these plants and animals. They probably also relied on beans and squash, but because these leave few traces in the archaeological record, we cannot be sure of their importance. The Pajaritans certainly depended on turkeys and maize, both of which can be tended in small areas and both of which make tasty, substantial meals. We conclude from the evidence of intensive farming and turkey rearing that hunting and gathering had lost some of their productivity on the plateau, because of the larger number of people living there.

A Change of Menu in the Classic Period

In the Classic period (1325–1600 CE) we see the establishment of large pueblos such as Tshirege, Tsankawi, and Otowi on the Pajarito Plateau, with smaller pueblos dotting the landscape. It might be assumed that people's aggregating into larger villages went hand in hand with population growth and an even greater concentration on agriculture. But surprisingly, during the Classic period the population of the Pajarito got progressively smaller, and the Pajaritans appear increasingly to have supplemented farming with the gathering of native plants.

What might have caused this shift? In a word, drought. The shortage of rain and snow throughout the 1400s and 1500s must have made dry farming difficult. Farmers moved their fields from the overworked mesa tops at higher elevations to the fresher soils of lower mesas and narrow canyon bottoms, but at the peril of receiving even less rainfall. A few canyon bottoms, such as that of Frijoles Canyon, offered permanent water, but the amount of usable land shrank dramatically. Between dwindling land and deepening drought, farming became a risky business. The Pajaritans were forced to change their eating habits and again turned to wild plants and the pioneer plants that grew in fields and around the pueblos.

We know from ethnographic accounts that Pueblo people used many gathered plants in their meals, for variety and taste as well as nutritional balance. For example, they ate piñon nuts, an important source of protein and fats, either raw or roasted. They collected juniper berries and heated them to make them taste better (they are otherwise quite bitter). People ate chokecherries fresh in summer and dried them for the winter. They picked other berries, such as wild strawberries, raspberries, and gooseberries, eating them in season and drying some for later use. They added berries

Figure 5.5. Sorting corn at Cochiti Pueblo, about 1905.

from the lemonade bush (squawbush) to water to make a lemon-flavored drink. Cactus fruits were roasted to remove the spines, and yucca fruits were prepared by boiling or roasting. The leaves of pigweed, goosefoot, beeweed, and prairie clover were boiled like spinach, and these, too, were sometimes dried for winter use. Pueblo people harvested the seeds of pigweed, goosefoot, and purslane and parched them in shallow pots, grinding them into a flour that could be used in many ways. They did this, too, with seeds of several types of native grasses, such as Indian rice grass and sand dropseed. Plants such as wild onion and saltbush were especially sought after for flavoring. Considering the ancestral ties binding the modern Tewa and Keresan pueblos and the villages of the Pajarito Plateau, we believe these ethnographic accounts of food preparation surely tell us that Pajaritans in earlier times used similar ingredients and methods of preparation.

Just at the time when we suspect farming was

ebbing in importance—that is, during the Classic period—we find increasing quantities of deer and turkey bones in Pajarito sites. Although the local deer population had undoubtedly been reduced in earlier times, Pajaritans still had access to the game-rich Jemez Mountains. Perhaps hunting and raising turkeys became more important during the Classic period as ways not only to supply food but also to acquire products to trade with people from the lowlands, whose access to flowing water for irrigation made them more likely to have agricultural produce to exchange.

By the mid-1500s, the plateau stood all but empty. Despite their tactics of diversification, people began to leave, seeking new homes where land was available and conditions were more inviting. Many relocated to the Rio Grande Valley, founding the Tewa and Keresan pueblos that thrive there today. Why did this happen during the so-called Classic period? All answers point to the impossibility of making a living in the face of both cultural and environmental stresses. The growing human population on the plateau gradually exhausted its arable land, and farmers could no longer grow enough maize to feed everyone. Though the people turned once more to the wild foods that had sustained them for millennia, in good times and bad, the lengthy droughts, together with changes in the landscape created by farming, had diminished those resources, too. The Parajito Plateau could no longer feed its people.

Kari M. Schmidt is a doctoral candidate at the University of New Mexico and an archaeologist with the Cultural Resources Team at Los Alamos National Laboratory. Meredith H. Matthews is a specialist in macrobotanical analysis and co-director of the Cultural Resources Management Program at San Juan College in Farmington, New Mexico.

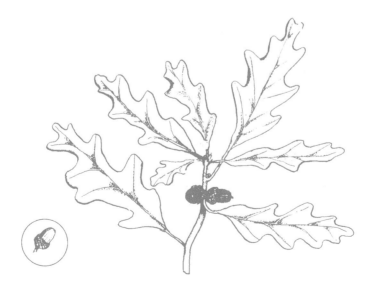

Figure 6.1. Big Kiva, Frijoles Canyon.

Creating the Pueblo Landscape of Bandelier, Stone by Stone

Tineke Van Zandt

On my first visit to Bandelier National Monument, I eagerly followed the interpretive trail up Frijoles Canyon to Tyuonyi Pueblo with its circle of excavated rooms, its kivas, and its large plaza. I hiked up to the cavates and scaled the ladders into Alcove House. Like most visitors to Bandelier, I was impressed and full of questions about what I had seen. I was not surprised that the Pueblo people had chosen to live in this beautiful oasis, but why had they eventually left? How many people lived in Frijoles Canyon, and when did they live there? And succumbing to my avid interest in local—or what I call "vernacular"—architecture, I wondered how the Puebloans had built and used the rooms, kivas, and plazas composing these villages.

It was only when I returned the following year as a member of the park's archaeological survey crew that I realized how limited my questions had been—I had seen only Frijoles Canyon. As we explored the fifty-plus square miles that make up the Bandelier backcountry, I began to see that Frijoles Canyon was very different from the rest of the monument. Puebloan farmers colonized the southern Pajarito Plateau in the 1100s, but most of Frijoles Canyon's inhabitants moved there some three hundred years later. In Frijoles, people lived in the canyon bottom in densely packed masonry and cavate pueblos, but elsewhere in the monument they rarely inhabited canyon bottoms. During their first 150 years there, they lived in tiny pueblos scat-

tered across the mesa tops. Once I started surveying, I quickly realized that pueblos bigger than twenty rooms were uncommon.

All of this was a revelation. I had missed the most intriguing questions of all: Why did the Pajaritans live in small pueblos first and then move into large villages? How did people cope with the move into larger settlements?

To answer my questions, I want to describe Puebloan architecture, the ways Puebloans placed their settlements in the Bandelier landscape, and how and why their architecture and settlements changed over the course of 450 years. I discuss population and the environment, because Pueblo people faced all sorts of social and environmental pressures in building their communities and had to respond to them. The number of people rose and fell at different times in response to changing environmental opportunities and challenges, including the arrival of many immigrants from other parts of the Southwest. As the population grew, Puebloans in the Bandelier area began to move into larger and larger pueblos, sharing their homes with more and more people.

Archaeologists call such dramatic increases in the sizes of settlements *aggregation*. Aggregation took place throughout the northern Southwest during the late prehistoric period, and it had dramatic effects on people and their homes. We will see that it affected the way pueblos were constructed, changed the length of time villages were occupied,

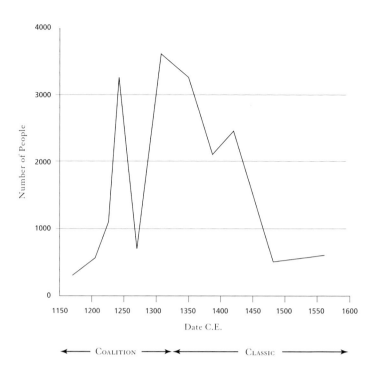

Figure 6.2. Estimated population in what is now Bandelier National Monument, 1150–1600 CE.

and altered the arrangement of communities across the landscape.

Moving In: 1150–1250 CE

Puebloan farmers began moving into what is now Bandelier National Monument around 1150 CE. Few people had lived anywhere on the Pajarito Plateau before that time, and population in the adjacent Rio Grande Valley was almost as sparse. Some of the new settlers were probably Chacoans arriving from the west, and others came from Mesa Verde, to the north. Perhaps some of these newcomers began to colonize the plateau because its forested mesas offered all the essentials of life: wood, game, building stone, water, and arable land. As tree-ring records show, higher elevations on the Pajarito Plateau received substantial rainfall, promising good opportunities for small-scale farming.

At first the settlers in Bandelier were few. Most people lived in tiny pueblos, or hamlets, each of about six to twelve rooms, home to some fifteen to thirty people. The rooms of these modest settlements were built of volcanic tuff blocks set in adobe mortar, arranged in a single block, two rooms wide.

When we find a hamlet like this on survey, the artifacts, mainly sherds of broken pottery and debris from stone tool making, are scattered over an area to the east or southeast of the pueblo. This was where people discarded their household garbage and their broken and worn-out items. Between the refuse dump and the pueblo lies an open space that served as an outdoor work area. These spaces were the forerunners of the plazas of later pueblos, but at this point they were small, unenclosed, and the products of daily use rather than intentional design. For this reason I hesitate to call them plazas. Inhabitants spent much of their time there, preparing food, cooking, making pots or arrow points, playing with their children, and even sleeping when the weather was good.

Sometimes these outdoor areas also encompass circular, underground structures known today as kivas, which were used for community religious ceremonies. The kivas' timber and earthen roofs probably extended slightly above ground level, and people entered them by means of a ladder descending through a hole in the chamber's roof. Most early kivas were quite small. One can estimate how many people used a kiva by looking at how many rooms there were in the nearby pueblo. Before 1250 the average was only twelve rooms per kiva. This combination—small kivas, only a few rooms in the pueblo, and a workspace rather than a formal plaza—suggests to me that early rituals brought together only a few families at a time.

The rooms facing the open work area were multipurpose living rooms that a single family used for many of the same things they did outside, especially when the weather was cold. Excavations show that these rooms usually had adobe floors with hearths and sometimes other built-in furniture such as storage bins. Behind each living room, and connected to it by doorways, lay one or two featureless rooms used mainly for storing the corn, beans, and squash so critical for survival over the winter. Each hamlet was composed of several of these nearly identical residential modules.

Figure 6.4. The wall of a small pueblo roughly built of locally available volcanic tuff.

Each pueblo probably housed a few related families who farmed in the immediate vicinity. At their more distant fields the families put up small, one- or two-room field houses so that they would have shelter and a place to store tools while tending their crops. Most hamlets were abandoned after a generation, likely because people had used up the resources in the surrounding area and depleted the soil. At that point, the families moved and built a new pueblo in a virgin location.

Casa del Rito, a small, early pueblo, is an excellent example of such a short-lived hamlet. Archaeologist Tim Kohler of Washington State University excavated Casa del Rito and found that its inhabitants had lived there for only about fifteen years, probably typical of most pueblos of the time. When its residents moved, they took all their possessions with them—even the roof beams. Clearly, they did not move far. Because the builders of this small pueblo expected to live in it only briefly, they had no incentive to put a great deal of effort into its construction. They were practical, and their simple, rough masonry reflects this.

After about 1220 CE, the number of Puebloans living in what is now Bandelier National Monument began to increase dramatically, an increase destined to have profound effects on both the existing population

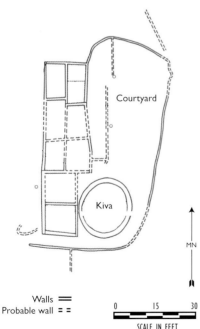

Walls ▬
Probable wall ▪ ▪

Courtyard

Kiva

MN

0   15   30
SCALE IN FEET

Figure 6.3. Aerial view and plan of Casa del Rito.

and the new arrivals. One striking feature of the years between 1220 and 1250 is that the rate of population growth was far greater than could have been achieved through natural increase alone—that is, through people's having children and grandchildren. Immigration from other places appears to have swelled the ranks.

Immigration took place not only at Bandelier and on the Pajarito Plateau but throughout the Rio Grande region. To understand where these immigrants came from, it is helpful to look at the general movement of people throughout the northern Southwest. One enduring question is, What happened to the inhabitants of Mesa Verde? From recent research in the Mesa Verde area, we think people began leaving there in the early 1200s and continued to do so until everyone was gone by 1280. Meanwhile, population grew in the Rio Grande region as a whole in the early 1200s and peaked after 1290, in almost a mirror image of the Four Corners pattern.

Although these matching departure and arrival dates are suggestive, one might well ask whether any corroborative evidence exists. Unfortunately, tracing population movements is tricky, especially when people move long distances and bring no distinctive household items with them for archaeologists to see as links. The Mesa Verdeans did, however, bring with them ideas. As it turns out, they had distinctive beliefs about how kivas should be made and furnished, ideas visibly different from those of people already living in the Rio Grande Valley.

Most northern Rio Grande kivas, for example, featured no interior bench or southern recess, and the firepit, deflector, and ventilator shaft were aligned toward the east. Mesa Verde kivas, in contrast, had a bench in a southern recess and a southern orientation. Two excavated kivas at Bandelier were built to these Mesa Verdean ideals. One of them was constructed between 1150 and 1200 CE, and the other, originally a Rio Grande–style kiva, was remodeled into a Mesa Verde–style kiva sometime in the early 1200s. Although these two are the only Mesa Verde–style kivas known so far on the Pajarito Plateau, they clearly point to the arrival of immigrants from the Four Corners.

As newcomers arrived, the landscape began to fill up with small pueblos, until moving was no longer an easy option. Rather than establish new settlements, many immigrants joined existing ones, and the pueblos grew larger, though none yet exceeded one hundred rooms. Perhaps existing pueblos had good stores of food, accumulated in bountiful times for emergency use during droughts, and were willing to share. The climate between 1220 and 1250 was favorable, so it is not surprising that settlements could have accommodated more people. Stores of surplus food, though, were only one incentive for people to move into larger pueblos. Because larger communities are forced to develop more effective ways of organizing themselves, their residents are better able to reduce competition over farmland by developing new ways of distributing land among themselves and establishing bounded territories to protect farmland from interlopers.

And there are other advantages to living in a larger pueblo: they attract trade and offer greater protection from conflict. Communities create ways to resolve interpersonal disputes. Living in a larger group means that people have more opportunities for ceremonies and religious observances, and some residents are able to specialize in making pottery, perhaps, or in weaving. Because of these advantages, people join the largest pueblos when they can, with the result that a few settlements grow especially rapidly. There are also disadvantages, especially crowding, quarrels, and much longer trips to and from fields. Nevertheless, in the minds of the Pajaritans, old and new, the advantages must have outweighed the disadvantages. Their pueblos grew to house from 30 to 180 people—many more than the earlier hamlets.

So far I have mentioned only individual settlements, but another way of understanding how people lived in Bandelier is to see how pueblos and communities were spread over the landscape. Shortly after the Bandelier area was colonized, pueblos were scattered so that no more than three or four sat close to one another (see plate 8). Few field houses existed, and they tended to be near the pueblos. People in neighboring hamlets would have seen each other frequently, and their settlements probably constituted small communities. This pattern continued through the early 1200s.

By 1235 to 1250 the population hit its first peak, and so did aggregation. We now see a pattern of settlement very different from that of the mid-1100s (see plate 9). Puebloan settlers by this time occupied a much larger portion of Bandelier and were joining in larger, multipueblo communities, mostly on mesa tops. Even though people still put up field houses near their pueblos, they also built them as much as a mile away. But we still see fairly small communities—small in numbers of people, in numbers of pueblos composing them, and in the area covered by each one.

Settling Down: 1250–1325 CE

The next three or four generations experienced huge changes in life at Bandelier. The decades from 1250 to 1290 saw an abrupt drop in population followed by a rapid rise through 1325. How can we account for these population changes?

From 1250 to 1290, the weather was very dry, and farmers may have struggled to grow crops successfully. The rapid depopulation of Bandelier at this time most likely represents a temporary relocation of people to places outside the present-day monument itself, either to higher elevations with more rain and snow or to places with permanent water, such as along the Rio Grande. Bandelier National Monument makes up only a small piece of the Pajarito Plateau and the Rio Grande Valley, and this population movement, local and temporary, did not affect the entire region.

During this short period of depopulation, the population pressures and weather conditions that had begun to favor people's aggregating in larger pueblos began to let up. The few people left in Bandelier no longer felt the need to live together, and they went back to small pueblos. Essentially, people returned to the way of life their ancestors had followed a hundred years earlier.

Environmental conditions improved after 1290. Renewed rainfall again allowed people to accumulate food surpluses, and once more Puebloans moved back into Bandelier. The population grew even more rapidly than before. Although some of the new arrivals may come from the south and west, as we see from the appearance of glaze-ware pottery making in the area, most still came

from the Mesa Verde region. Oddly, these post-1290 migrants did not build Mesa Verde–style kivas. Although this is puzzling at first, we can understand their situation better by looking at the overall nature of migration in the late 1200s.

Most people left the Mesa Verde region in small family groups, not as entire villages or communities. But whereas early immigrants had moved into a sparsely populated landscape, those of the 1200s were entering an already inhabited territory. The first immigrants simply brought their religious building styles and practices to the new land. The later arrivals had to integrate themselves into existing communities in order to be accepted, get access to farmland, take part in trade networks, find eligible marriage partners, and contribute to rituals. The need to fit in probably led them deliberately to deemphasize old practices such as building distinctive kivas. They might also have consciously abandoned aspects of Pueblo ritual that were seen as responsible for the failure of village life in their Mesa Verde homeland.

Even though more and more Puebloans were now living in Bandelier, some people chose to continue dwelling in small pueblos. Others began, once again, to move into larger, aggregated settlements. Whether in small or large pueblos, however, people began to live longer in one place. As pueblos became larger and more permanent, their builders made notable changes in architecture and design that define the first true villages. During our survey, whenever we discovered one of these large pueblos, I knew I was in for a challenge. As the architectural specialist on the crew, I was the one responsible for drawing the ground plan, and it was often complicated.

The reason it was complicated to draw the outline of such a pueblo lay in the efforts the prehistoric builders had made to solve their emerging housing crisis. Abandoning the old style of modular residences, they began to build the largest pueblos with at least three blocks, or wings, of rooms; some even had four roomblocks connected at right angles to form a hollow square surrounding a central plaza. These plaza pueblos were much more common, and often larger and more elaborate, on the northern Pajarito Plateau than in Bandelier.

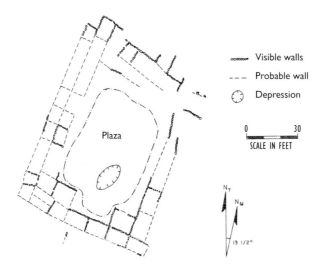

Legend:
- ∞∞∞ Visible walls
- - - - Probable wall
- ◯ Depression

0   30
SCALE IN FEET

13 1/2°

Figure 6.5. Plan of a plaza pueblo, late 1200s.

Most of the new pueblos were also wider—that is, they contained significantly more rows of rooms—so that each village was capable of housing more people and storing more food. A second innovation was the construction of upper stories. The largest pueblos, including the ones with plazas, usually had second-story rooms. With all of these changes, residential suites grew larger, more irregular, and more vertical —and harder to recognize archaeologically.

Puebloan builders made other changes in large pueblo designs as a result of their desire to live in one place for longer periods. Excavation evidence clearly shows that the longer a pueblo was inhabited, the more its occupants refurbished and renovated it. They not only remodeled individual rooms by repairing roof beams, replastering walls and floors, and adding or dismantling hearths and storage bins, but they also added entire blocks of new rooms. Without archaeological excavation, most remodeling is invisible, but additions of entire rooms or blocks often make a pueblo's layout noticeably more irregular.

Another obvious and important change was that Puebloan builders began to use carefully shaped stones in the walls of rooms. Shaped masonry provides a stronger, more stable platform for building upper stories, but it was used even for single-story construction. This implies that the use of shaped tuff blocks was not simply a practical matter but

reflected a conscious decision by Puebloan builders to construct homes that would be used by future generations.

Social and ritual architecture began to evolve, too. Although the sizes of kivas remained constant, the number of rooms associated with each kiva more than doubled, from an average of twelve rooms per kiva before 1250 to almost thirty after that date. This implies that more people were using each kiva. After 1290, the first formal plazas appeared, enclosed on three or four sides by rooms. These plazas were multifunctional spaces, sites of everyday tasks as well as rituals. Both types of activities played important roles in bringing all the members of the village together. When plazas were used for rituals, we can imagine that virtually the entire village participated, either as performers or as observers lining the edges of the plaza and the adjacent rooftops, just as they do today in modern pueblos.

The overall spread of settlements across the landscape during this time of rapid growth and large pueblo construction was much like what we saw for the early 1200s, but multipueblo communities were now even more pronounced (see plate 10). Each community cluster contained both small and large pueblos, at least one of them a new large pueblo. Although only one of these pueblos boasts more than a hundred rooms, and some lack a kiva, each community had at least one kiva. And at least one pueblo, usually centrally located, surrounded a plaza. This suggests that the pueblos with kivas or plazas served as community gathering places. The architectural and design changes displayed in these new pueblos—folding family suites into large, multistoried roomblocks, putting more people into a few kivas, and constructing large plazas suitable for community ceremonies—signal the end of old social divisions and the birth of unified settlements that were truly villages. One of the earliest of these large community pueblos was the village of Yapashi.

Fewer People and Bigger Pueblos: 1325–1550 CE

After 1325, the number of Puebloans living on the southern Pajarito Plateau began to diminish. One

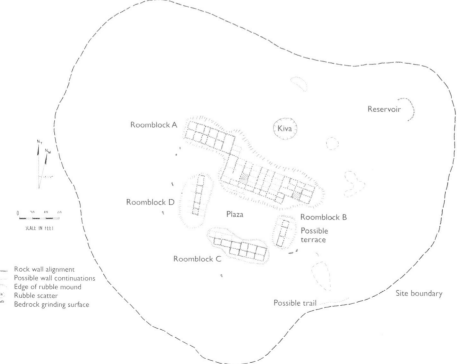

Roomblock A

Kiva

Reservoir

Roomblock D

Plaza

Roomblock B

Possible terrace

Roomblock C

0   20   40   60
SCALE IN FEET

Rock wall alignment
Possible wall continuations
Edge of rubble mound
Rubble scatter
Bedrock grinding surface

Possible trail

Site boundary

Figure 6.6. Aerial view and plan of San Miguel Pueblo.

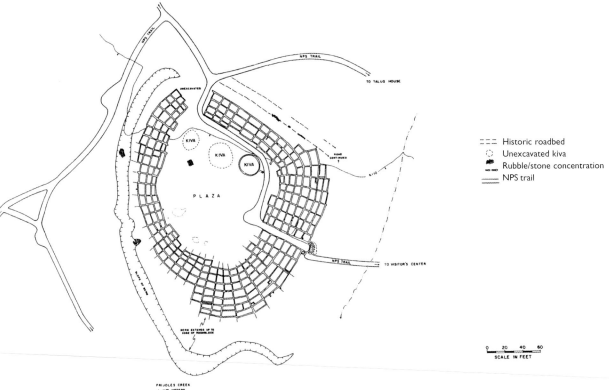

=== Historic roadbed
○ Unexcavated kiva
Rubble/stone concentration
NPS trail

Figure 6.7. Aerial view and plan of Tyuonyi Pueblo, showing its unusual circular shape.

Figure 6.8. Big Kiva, Frijoles Canyon.

reason might be that people who had resisted joining the large villages were finally forced to move
away, because they were denied access to good
agricultural land or trade goods now under village
control. The majority of people stayed, however,
and moved into the large pueblos, or "community
houses," as some early archaeologists called them.
The concentration of people in large villages peaked
between 1375 and 1440, some fifty to one hundred
years after the population began to drop. Although
the weather stayed favorable for farming until
about 1375, after that time Puebloans faced more
frequent and often longer droughts. They spaced
their pueblos evenly across the landscape, probably
to lessen competition over land and game. As
droughts made agriculture increasingly difficult,
villages by the permanent water supply of the Rio
Grande became increasingly attractive as places to
move to, and population continued to ebb.

By the time the large pueblos reached their
zenith, dry weather no longer really provided a
motive for aggregating, but the remaining Puebloans
stayed on in them, especially in Frijoles Canyon,
when they could easily have dispersed. This continued use of large pueblos, despite fewer people
and poorer environmental conditions, suggests that
Pajaritans decide to stay largely for social reasons.
Even when they finally abandoned the Pajarito

Plateau altogether, they joined other large villages
in the Rio Grande Valley rather than returning to
the small pueblo lifestyle of their ancestors.

After 1325 Puebloans continued to expand
upon their new architectural and design methods.
They built large pueblos with roomblocks enclosing
one or more plazas; each roomblock encompassed
multiple rows of rooms, now two to four stories
tall. People built with an abundance of carefully
shaped tuff blocks, which clearly were more time
consuming to prepare. Tyuonyi Pueblo is a good
example of such a village. Although its circular
shape is unusual, it displays other characteristics
of large pueblos.

By modern standards, a community of several
hundred people is small, but these villages were
several times larger than any previous pueblos on
the Pajarito Plateau. More neighbors means less
privacy; it also means having more people to dis-
agree with, and disputes between neighbors must
have been common. Anthropologists think that
one role of ritual is to ease friction and help people
get along: we call it "ritual integration." The elabo-
ration of ritual architecture on the plateau suggests
that village inhabitants coped with some social
stresses through rituals and ceremonies that helped
them grapple with the realities of living so close
together.

One of the most visible developments was the enlargement of kivas to nearly 550 square feet apiece, about three times their former size. More people now fit into each kiva, and the average of almost seventy village rooms per kiva indicates that more than twice as many people now used each chamber. The largest pueblos in Bandelier, including Tsankawi, Tyuonyi, and Yapashi, each had more than three hundred rooms and multiple kivas. Villages such as Otowi and Puye on the northern Pajarito Plateau were even larger. At each of these pueblos, residents also constructed one supersize kiva known as a "big" kiva. The three known big kivas average nearly fifteen hundred square feet. In Frijoles Canyon, the residents of Tyuonyi and several nearby canyon-floor pueblos, as well as those of all the cavate pueblos, shared a single supersize kiva appropriately named Big Kiva.

An equally important space for ceremonies, present at every pueblo with ninety rooms or more, was the fully enclosed plaza. In the large pueblos the plazas were more than five times larger than those of earlier times. Taking each of these architectural features into account, we can see that Puebloan villages had three levels of ritual architecture: small

kivas used by small groups such as clans or religious societies, a big kiva used by representatives of the many kiva groups, and a plaza used for community-wide rituals in which everybody participated.

The increased size and importance of plazas after 1325 likely reflected the growing importance of the katsina religion. The system of beliefs known as the katsina cult developed elsewhere in the Southwest, arriving in the northern Rio Grande region sometime in the late 1200s or early 1300s. Although the katsina religion, still practiced by modern Pueblo people, includes rituals carried out inside kivas, katsina dances are performed publicly in the plaza. These dances involve the entire village, either as dancers or as spectators, and include community-wide feasts. Clowns, who, unlike Western clowns, are religious figures, publicly ridicule antisocial behavior. Katsina ritual is a powerful unifying force that helps people feel they are working toward common goals with shared values.

The concentration of people into a few large villages had completely changed the settlement landscape of the Pajarito Plateau by the end of the 1300s (see plate 11). Large pueblos were evenly spaced across the terrain. Interestingly, each large pueblo sat near the center of one of the settlement clusters of the late 1200s, suggesting continuity in community membership despite change in the community's physical character. Fields were scattered over the broad mesa tops between the pueblos, and field houses became much more numerous and more necessary, even though only few of them can be dated to the 1375–1400 interval illustrated in plate 11. Some now lay more than three miles from the nearest pueblo. Because of these distances, some families probably spent all summer at their field houses. Doing so might have relieved some of the stresses of crowded pueblo life, although farmers and their families probably visited the pueblo to attend summer katsina dances.

During the late 1400s, population on the Pajarito Plateau fell precipitously, but the arrangement of widely spaced villages survived into the early 1500s (see plate 12). As population shrank, each village housed fewer people, and the remaining residents must have been surrounded by vacant

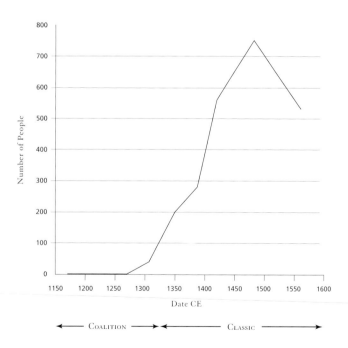

Figure 6.9. Estimated population in Frijoles Canyon alone, 1150–1600 CE.

or ruined rooms. After 1525 the only people left in Bandelier were those living in places with permanent water, such as Frijoles Canyon. Frijoles appears to have held onto a substantial number of residents until about 1550; by 1600 it was largely uninhabited.

What happened to the Pajaritans? Eventually the last families living in the mostly empty villages decided to go elsewhere. Some, perhaps most, moved to the Rio Grande Valley, where they joined the residents of other large pueblos. Three centuries later, Adolph Bandelier heard vivid stories from residents of Cochiti about the emigration of their ancestors southward from Bandelier (see chapter 12). Those Pajaritans who lived north of Frijoles Canyon moved east to San Juan and San Ildefonso Pueblos. Descendants of the people who once lived in Bandelier still make their homes in these villages.

A New Foundation

The questions I posed at the beginning of this chapter have complex answers. After several years of studying the architecture and settlement patterns of Bandelier's Puebloan residents, I have come to recognize that buildings, population, and environment are all related. In combination they yield insights into how the ancient Puebloans made decisions about where to live, how long to remain, how many other people to live with, how to build their houses, and how to get along with each other. Bandelier's inhabitants did not simply react mechanically to changes in the environment or in population size; they created novel ways for more people to live together. Waves of immigration, a changing climate, new architectural designs, and a strong religious system provided the ingredients for new kinds of villages. These ingredients included new ceremonial structures and community organizations as well as new ways of using the landscape. The Parajitans' lifestyle succeeded for more than four hundred years, and even though their innovations ultimately fell short of allowing them to stay on the plateau, they formed the foundation of modern-day Pueblo society.

Tineke Van Zandt was a member of the Bandelier Archaeological Survey and is chair of the Department of Social Sciences at Pima Community College in Tucson, Arizona.

Figure 7.1. This animated figure near Tsankawi Pueblo is difficult to spot but appears to be waving in greeting.

Bringing the Rocks to Life

seven

Marit K. Munson

The rocks have come alive. Moments earlier, tired visitors on the main interpretive trail in Bandelier National Monument had stopped in front of the cliff at Long House. Scanning the cliff for the rock art promised in their trail guides, doubt visible in their hot faces, they are about to move on. And then someone spots a face, then a snake, then a set of circles pecked into the cliff. Energized, the visitors grin cheerfully and point out images to their companions: a person with arms upraised as if in greeting, a turkey, a dog—or is it a coyote? Dozens of images emerge, an encounter all the more delightful for being unexpected. In just a moment, the blank expanse of rock has been transformed into a window onto another world.

The images we see on the cliffs of the Pajarito Plateau—both petroglyphs, which are pecked into rocks, and pictographs, which are painted on them—give us a sense of connection. They bring the past to life—the everyday events of Pueblo ancestors who raised their children and buried their dead, tended farms and prayed for rain, danced in rituals and drew pictures on the cliffs. A petroglyph can seem to greet us directly from the past and promise a glimpse into the minds of ancient artists. But understanding these images is much more difficult than it first seems.

Some early explorers in the Southwest tried to decipher the rock art, believing it was a form of writing. Others, like Adolph Bandelier, thought of rock art as a mere curiosity. The archaeologist Edgar Lee Hewett initially found rock carvings deeply symbolic of ancient Pueblo religion but then had a change of heart and dismissed them as "crude" and "uninteresting." And Gustave Baumann, the German-American artist known for his woodcuts of the Grand Canyon, Taos, and Santa Fe, found in Pajarito rock art the inspiration for an entire book of prints.

Today, we question whether or not *rock art* is even an appropriate term for these pecked or painted images. The term art brings to mind an artist, perhaps even an unappreciated genius, creating works that will one day be displayed in galleries and museums. But petroglyphs and pictographs are immobile, permanently fixed in relationship to the

Figure 7.2. Gustave Baumann drew inspiration from the rock art of Bandelier for woodblock prints he made in the 1920s and 1930s.

land around them. If they are removed from their original locations, or if their surroundings are disrupted, that relationship is destroyed. Pueblo people made rock art not simply for self-expression or as something to be admired; they probably made much of it for religious purposes. If prayers for rain are central to the lives of farmers in a desert, can a petroglyph of a rain cloud be "just" art? Or is it part of something greater? I use the term rock art for want of another word that is descriptive but not unwieldy. Regardless of what we call these images, regardless of whether they are religious or secular, all rock art is now a cherished part of Pueblo heritage. As such, it is worthy of respect and protection.

What Is It?

Rock art from Bandelier and other parts of the Pajarito Plateau includes a dizzying array of images and forms. Geometric shapes such as zigzags, concentric circles, and lines dot the cliffs, interspersed with images of humans and animals. Some of them are easy to identify: turkeys, snakes, deer, mountain lions. In other cases it is difficult even to tell the

Visiting Rock Art Sites

Rock art sites are more than just the petroglyphs —they include the rocks, the area around them, even the view. As you look, remember that rock art, despite its apparent permanence, is actually quite fragile. The soft tuff in Bandelier National Monument is susceptible to crumbling or being worn away by a casual touch. Even hard basalt can be damaged over time by a visitor's hands. Do not attempt to add anything to the rock art to make it easier to see. People used to highlight the images by drawing around them with chalk, but this, too, can cause damage. It's a good idea to bring binoculars when visiting a site; by focusing your attention, they can help you find images you might otherwise miss. Rock art can be almost invisible in certain light, so patience is truly a virtue.

difference between a bird and a mammal. Then there are the downright puzzling depictions. What can we make of limbless people with square heads and boxy bodies? Or a person with a giant X across its body? Why are men holding flutes often shown with erect penises? Why do some people have enormous round bodies with detailed decoration? Why would a snake have horns? What are antlers doing on a creature with a mountain lion's body?

We can suggest reasonable answers to some of these questions through analogy with the Pueblo Indians today. For example, images of people with kilts, horns, fancy hairstyles, or patterned faces and bodies may show dancers who represent supernatural beings, similar to the katsina dancers in historic Pueblo ceremonies. Or these images might be pictures of deities themselves. Snakes with horns probably depict the horned serpents that guard springs. The round-bodied humans are similar to those in detailed prehistoric paintings from kivas, or ceremonial rooms, that show warriors holding large shields. As for the phallic figures, suffice it to say that it is easy to imagine some bragging or joking going on. And before I give the impression that this was just among the men, I should add that there are images of women with genitals, too. Of course, including such details might simply have been a way of showing whether the figures were men or women; sometimes, a penis is just a penis.

How Old Is It?

Rock art is notoriously difficult to date. The methods that archaeologists use for other purposes, such as tree-ring dating and radiocarbon dating, are not feasible for rock art. For my work at Bandelier I used an indirect dating method called stylistic seriation. Seriation is the ordering of designs or forms in a sequence that displays gradual change—somewhat like arranging cars from the Model T to the SUV. It works under the assumption that the style, or appearance, of the rock art has changed through time, just as the size of a Cadillac's fins change according to fashion. The trick is to figure out which stylistic traits gained popularity and then fell into disuse, and which traits were more constant. This is hard to do by hand for thousands of images, so I used a statistical method called correspondence

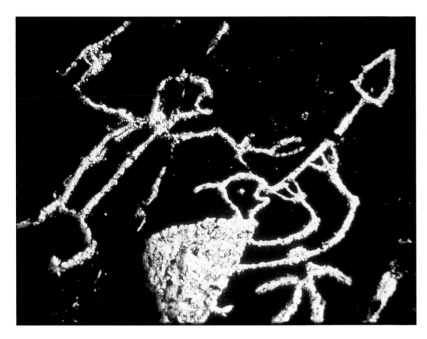

Figure 7.3. An arrow swallower scratched into the black sooted wall of a cavate in Mortandad Canyon.

site, between 1425 and 1550 CE. So Long House falls at the more recent end of the sequence, and sites from the 1200s lie at the earlier end.

How Has Rock Art Changed?

With a good seriation, we can begin to look at how the rock art of the Pajarito Plateau changed through time. Between about 1175 and 1325 CE, for example, artists pecked solid human figures with simple, naturalistic bodies, necks, feet, legs, and arms; they seldom added other details, although some figures are shown with feathers on their heads. A few humans have short lines like horns on their heads, and others have small circles at the side of the head—perhaps ears or the hair whorls that Pueblo women traditionally wore. The creators occasionally added what may represent headdresses, as in a human wearing horns with balls on their tips or a figure with rabbitlike ears. Flute players are quite common. Solidly pecked and shown in profile, they usually have straight flutes, humped backs, and phalluses. They are often shown with bent legs, as if they are seated or dancing.

Sometime in the early 1300s, striking changes in rock art accompanied the beginning of what is known as the Classic period. Classic artists depicted humans in a new geometric form. Although they continued to create some figures in the solidly pecked naturalistic style of the earlier period, most artists now carefully outlined square or rectangular bodies and heads, drawing them with precise angles. The artists must have had the specific configuration of the shoulders and upper body in mind before they began to create the fine outline, because they left the top of the body open where it linked to the distinct "hollow" neck. Many human figures were pared down to an abstract set of geometric shapes and precise lines; some included details such as facial features, feathers, headdresses, and geometric lines on their torsos. The phallic men so common in earlier rock art became rare in the Classic period;

analysis to help me look systematically for stylistic changes in rock art depictions of human figures. This analysis highlighted the traits, such as certain head or body shapes, that tended to occur together. It also placed the rock art sites in order on the basis of stylistic similarities among sites. Sites with the most stylistically similar rock art probably date to the same time period, whereas those with little in common are more widely separated in time. The problem is how to distinguish which end of the sequence is the oldest and which is the most recent.

In this endeavor I had an advantage over my colleagues studying rock art elsewhere: the Pajarito Plateau's cavate pueblos. Much of the rock art I studied was made by people standing on the roofs of rooms built against the cliff face. After the villages were abandoned, the buildings collapsed, leaving the rock art stranded two or three stories above ground level. This unusually close association between the rock art and the buildings means that the dates of the buildings are also the dates of the images. This in turn provides the independent evidence needed to properly set up the stylistic sequence. At Long House, for example, the vast majority of the rock art was made while the pueblo was still occupied—according to pottery from the

Figure 7.4. Coalition-period human figures.

when sex is indicated, the figure is usually a woman. Artists still made images of flute players, but they did so using abstract, looping lines completely unlike those in the earlier figures.

The artists of the early 1300s did not just change the style of the images they made; they also began to place their rock art in completely different places. Coalition-period rock art, made before about 1325, was almost all created on the interior walls of cavate rooms. As Angelyn Bass Rivera describes in chapter 11, many cavates have heavily sooted upper walls and ceilings, creating a solid black surface. The artists pecked through the soot, forming a high-contrast image by exposing the white or light gray tuff underneath. Cavates are quite small, so images placed on interior walls would have been visible to only a few people at a time—and even then, only to whomever the owner of the room cared to invite in. Rock art before about 1325 was a private affair, produced on a small scale for individual or family use. Even the occasional images that show up on cliff faces outside the cavates are seldom near villages or trails that were used daily.

Rock art after 1325, in contrast, could hardly be more visible. Cavate pueblos of the Classic period were full of public imagery, most of it made by artists standing on the rooftops. Ancient Pueblo people probably used the rooftops as convenient work spaces or pleasant spots in which to gather in fine weather, so every resident would have seen the cliff-face art regularly. This suggests that imagery after 1325 was more important to the village as a whole than to individuals. Remember, too, that this newly public rock art was made with greater care and in a more codified, geometric style than that of the previous period.

Why Did Rock Art Change?

What happened in the early 1300s to bring about such dramatic changes? The classic answer, given the historic boundary on the Pajarito Plateau between Keres and Tewa speakers, is that changes in rock art reflected artists' efforts to display their identity as members of one of these two groups. Indeed, other kinds of archaeological evidence suggest that the distinction between Keres and Tewa people might have been important by the early 1300s (see chapter 8). Yet a closer look at the context of rock art raises doubts that marking group boundaries or declaring linguistic identity was the artists' main goal.

Figure 7.5. Classic-period human figures.

Figure 7.6. A shield with star above the collapsed roof (note roof beam sockets) of a cliff-face room at Long House.

Figure 7.7. Sun symbol and a birdlike animal at the top of the sheer cliff overlooking Talus House.

First, the audience is all wrong. If people want to use rock art to communicate, they have to make sure the images are visible to those they want to reach. And though some petroglyphs may have served as trail markers, as James Snead describes in chapter 10, little of the Pajarito rock art appears in suitably "billboard"-like places. In other cases, the location is right but the image is hard to see. It is surprisingly easy to miss the sun symbol and bird-like animal above Talus House, for example, unless you have been warned to look for them. It appears that the people who lived in each cavate pueblo were the primary audience for most of the rock art.

In addition, the rock art varies from community to community. If artists had been trying to symbolize distinctive Keres or Tewa identities, then we might expect to see two different sets of rock art—images important to each artist's own group. Instead, each major pueblo, along with its smaller surrounding villages—regardless of language affiliation—seems to have expressed its own preference. In the area around Tsankawi Pueblo, for instance, artists frequently depicted flute players, thunderbirds, warlike images of shield bearers and weapons, and people swallowing arrows. Just a little to the southwest, at the large Classic pueblo of Tshirege, shields and concentric circles are common. Both pueblos lie north of the historic Keres-Tewa boundary in Frijoles Canyon, yet each emphasized its own distinct images.

Rock art in historic Keres territory, south of Frijoles Canyon, also varied. In Frijoles itself, simple pecked faces, concentric circles, and plain circles are typical. In southern Bandelier, near Painted Cave, artists often painted rather than pecked images onto the rocks. The artists' choices suggest that rock art reflected village concerns rather than a broader distinction between Keres and Tewa speakers.

What Does It Mean?

The meaning of rock art is a surprisingly difficult subject. We know from historic accounts of Pueblo religion that some images have sacred meanings. Imagery related to rain or moisture is linked to fertility, to the growth of crops, and therefore to life itself. Similarly, images of people with kilts, headdresses, rattles, and other accoutrements are tied to katsinas and katsina dancers. On a general level, then, rock art depicting rain clouds (in a traditional terrace shape), corn plants, and katsina dancers has religious meaning. Such images are plentiful in some parts of the Rio Grande Valley—at Petroglyph National Monument, for example, on Albuquerque's West Mesa. But few images of this sort appear in Bandelier or on the rest of the Pajarito Plateau, and those that exist seem to date to the historic period.

This presents something of a puzzle. We know that the ancient inhabitants of the Pajarito Plateau were the ancestors of some modern Pueblo people, yet the imagery from the two eras is so different. Is it possible that Pajarito rock art had no religious meaning at all? The answer is an unequivocal no. Large sites on the Pajarito often include a kind of secluded rock-art alcove, somewhat removed from the traffic of daily life. Each alcove contains several rock art panels, partly enclosed by cliff walls that define a small flat area, or platform. The artists covered the walls with images, overlapping them in a way that suggests heavy use of the alcove over time. The repeated creation of specific images in the same space has clear parallels to the historic Pueblo practice of refreshing murals on the walls of kivas or churches by periodically repainting them.

The secluded character of these spaces also finds parallels in the historic use of kivas, where ceremonies cannot be viewed by people who are not properly initiated. Indeed, many aspects of

Pueblo religious life are secret. Participation in rituals, care of sacred objects, and even access to certain kinds of religious knowledge are all carefully controlled.

If some of the ancient Pajarito images are religious, then why are they so different from historic images? To me, the shift in the style of human figures that took place in the early 1300s suggests a change in the beliefs of the artists making the rock art. The earlier human images, with their naturalistic forms, seem to be pictures of actual people. In contrast, the geometric, abstract style that artists used in the Classic period turned human figures into icons representing not persons but roles, perhaps, or mythical beings. Whereas Coalition-period artists often depicted shields, shield bearers, and other warlike images, Classic-period artists began to produce images that appear to have centered on supernaturals in human form. Artists also included some images that have parallels in historic Pueblo religion, such as the terraces that represent rain clouds and the macaws that provide brightly colored feathers for ceremonies and ritual clothing.

This shift toward humanlike (rather than human) imagery, along with the presence of elements that had religious significance historically, suggests that the inhabitants of Bandelier adopted a new religion in the early 1300s that centered on supernaturals in human form. Contemporaneous rock art and kiva murals from elsewhere in the Rio Grande Valley suggest that many other people in northern New Mexico did the same.

Whether or not these supernaturals were katsinas is difficult to say. Spirits in human form appear to have been a consistent part of Pueblo belief since at least the early 1300s, yet the rock art and pottery of the time bear few images with clear parallels to historic Pueblo katsinas. Perhaps the artists' view of these supernaturals changed over the centuries, or the way they represented them changed. Either way, archaeological evidence from the Pajarito Plateau indicates that some reasons for making rock art have remained constant. Pueblo artists created rock art for religious purposes at least as far back as the early 1300s. And although many Pueblo people are understandably reluctant to expose details of their private and religious

Figure 7.8. Two views of Painted Cave. Top, late 1800s; bottom, 1987, showing addition of a six-pointed star, and a large animal or monster head near the snake's head and tail.

activities to the world, historic photographs clearly show that artists continued to make rock art in Bandelier into the twentieth century.

Over the last millennium, some aspects of Pueblo culture have changed dramatically while others have endured. The rock art of the Pajarito Plateau offers a unique window onto this dynamic Pueblo world. With close attention and a respectful attitude, we can appreciate the skill of these artists, past and present, and catch a glimpse of their lives through the centuries.

Marit K. Munson is an archaeologist, a rock art special-ist, and a professor at Trent University in Ontario, Canada.

Figure 8.1. Cerro Pedernal, source of the chert gravels found on the northern Pajarito Plateau.

Plate 1. Aerial view of the Pajarito Plateau.

Plate 2. View of Frijoles Canyon.

Plate 3. Clovis points.

Plate 4. Woolly mammoth.

Plate 5. Corn plants growing in Frijoles Canyon.

Plate 6. Frijoles Creek.

Plate 7. Wild seeds characteristic of the Pajarito Plateau. Back row: yucca, opuntia, chokecherry; front row: Indian rice grass, tansy mustard, pigweed.

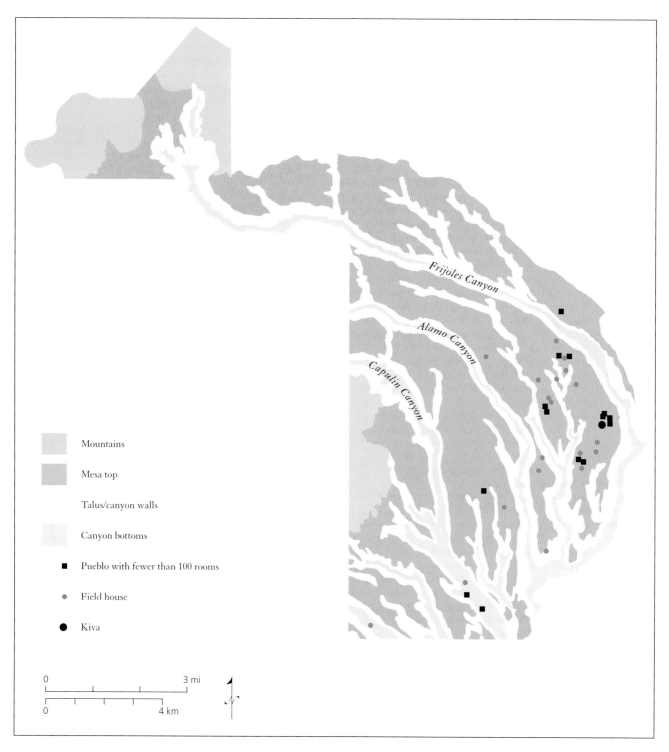

Frijoles Canyon

Alamo Canyon

Capulin Canyon

Mountains

Mesa top

Talus/canyon walls

Canyon bottoms

■ Pueblo with fewer than 100 rooms

● Field house

● Kiva

0   3 mi

0   4 km

N

Plate 8. Settlements in Bandelier between 1150 and 1190 CE.

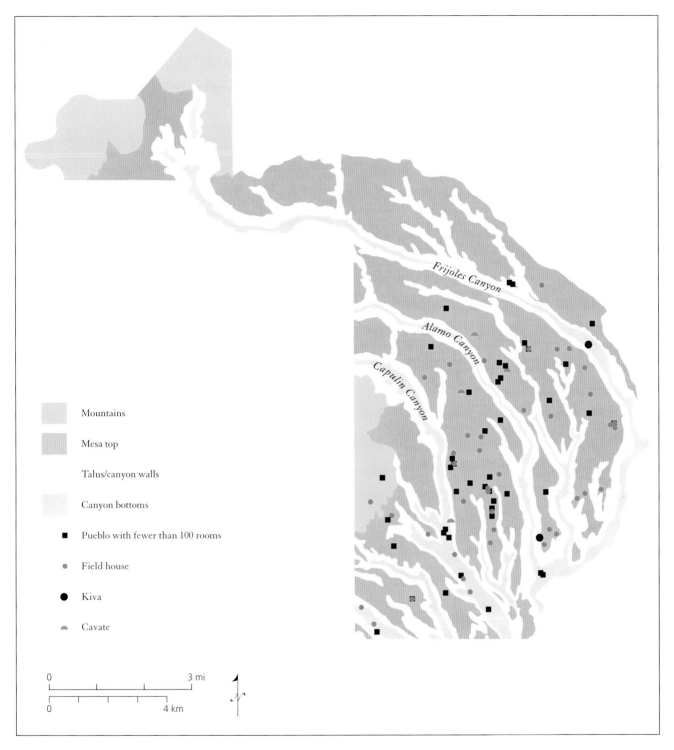

Plate 9. Settlements in Bandelier between 1235 and 1250 CE.

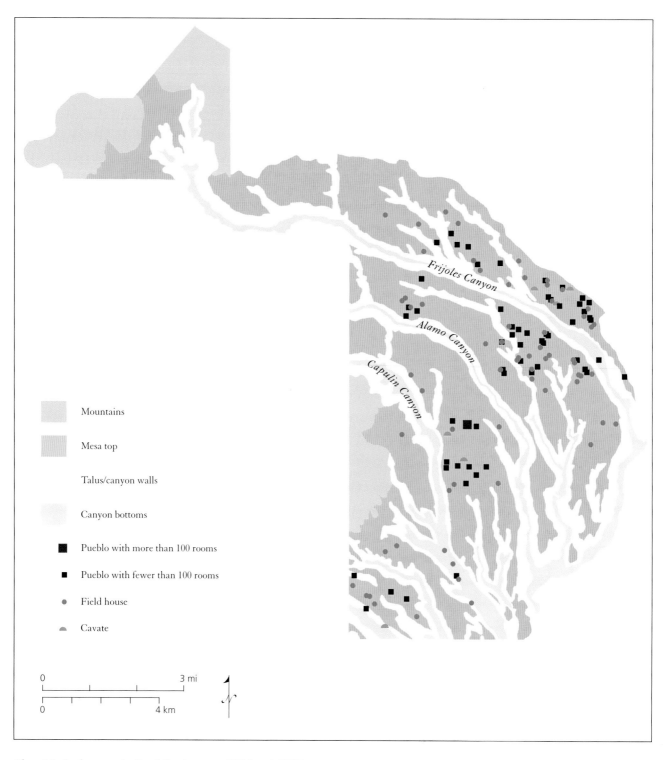

Legend (within map):

Mountains

Mesa top

Talus/canyon walls

Canyon bottoms

■ Pueblo with more than 100 rooms

■ Pueblo with fewer than 100 rooms

● Field house

◣ Cavate

Frijoles Canyon

Alamo Canyon

Capulin Canyon

0   3 mi

0   4 km

N

Plate 10. Settlements in Bandelier between 1290 and 1325 CE.

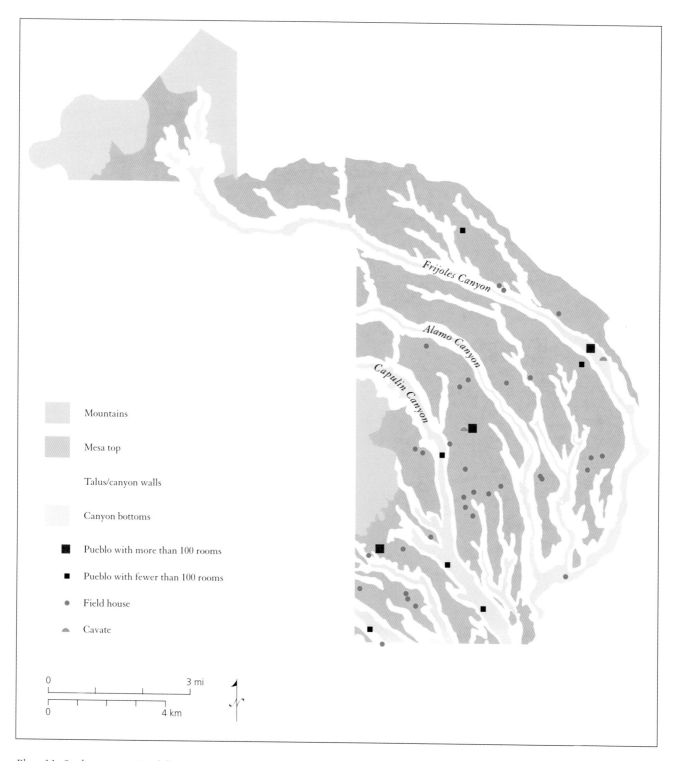

Plate 11. Settlements in Bandelier between 1375 and 1400 CE.

Frijoles Canyon

Alamo Canyon

Capulin Canyon

0   3 mi

0   4 km

Plate 12. Settlements in Bandelier between 1440 and 1525 CE.

Getting Blood from a Stone

Michael R. Walsh

Before metal, there was stone. Stone provided the raw material for tools used in hunting, harvesting, preparing food, defending oneself or one's family, and even rituals. Any job that required a sharp edge, a point, or a rough surface was done with stone. Archaeologists usually rely on stone tools as clues in understanding prehistoric technology and subsistence—how a hunter made arrowheads, whether a knife was used to cut wood, sinew, plants, or flesh, and how the shapes of grinding stones changed over years of use. When we reconstruct the social or political lifeways of ancient Puebloans, we are far more likely to turn to pottery and architecture—perhaps because these things are more familiar to us. But stone tools, too, are potential sources of information about many facets of prehistoric social and political organization, and I propose to explain why.

Prehistoric Pajaritan tool makers sought out certain kinds of stone for certain reasons, and I believe their choices of raw materials give us valuable information about ancient village territories. It may be a bold leap, but I think some of these territories on the Pajarito cleaved along a line that represents an ethnic boundary established centuries ago by the ancestors of the present-day Keres and Tewa Pueblo people. Because the plateau offers ample evidence of prehistoric uses of stone, and because we have modern knowledge of the historic Keres-Tewa boundary, I believe I can demonstrate how stones speak to us about changing prehistoric social relationships.

If stone tools are an important part of one's

daily life, then the Pajarito Plateau is a great place to live. Stone for flaking sharp-edged cutting and piercing tools or for shaping coarse grinding tools is generously available up and down the mesas and canyons. In this chapter I look solely at flaked stone tools and ignore ground stone tools such as manos and metates, for two reasons. First, archaeologists and geologists are able to pinpoint the sources of raw materials for flaked stone tools, and these sources are geographically local. A chert with certain distinctive qualities, for example, might outcrop in a single, geologically unique area, so any artifacts made of that recognizable chert had to have come from that source. Sources of stone suitable for ground stone tools are far more widespread and less easily isolated. Knowing where the raw materials came from is critical in analyzing stone tools. Second, flaked stone tools, and especially the debris left over

Figure 8.2. A grooved basalt tool used as a maul.

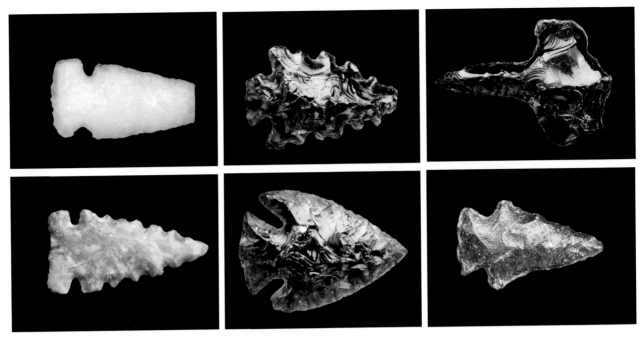

Figure 8.3. Well-made arrow points and a drill found in Bandelier National Monument.

from their manufacture, are extremely common artifacts on archaeological sites; ground stone tools are far fewer. Simply put, flaked stone, visible on the surface of virtually every site, provides a great deal of information, and ground stone tools do not.

The Pajaritans flaked a wide variety of tools out of stone, and these disclose interesting details about their lifeways. The sheer numbers of certain tools suggest that Puebloan farmers supplemented their meals of corn, beans, and squash with wild foods to a surprising degree. These tools include arrow points, of course. In the absence of any evidence for prehistoric warfare, we can assume they were used as hunting weapons. Additional tell-tale artifacts are scraping and cutting tools that people used to butcher animals, cut and gather plant foods, and prepare both plants and animals for consumption. The importance of wild resources in the diet is significant because it highlights the Pajaritans' need for hunting and gathering territories beyond the land required for agricultural fields.

Although the Pajaritans were skilled tool makers, their everyday stone technology was relatively simple, or "expedient." They shaped or modified many of their tools very little, but even minor modifications made the tools conveniently multifunctional. In every sense, Pajaritans made and carried

stone versions of the Swiss army knife. They also discarded many of their tools freely, often after completing just a single task. Such tools—expediently made and easily discarded—are characteristic of people who live where copious raw material is available and who collect the material firsthand, for personal use, rather than obtaining it through trade.

People who obtain materials firsthand likely get them through what we call an "embedded strategy"—they gather usable stone while doing other things such as hunting and gathering. This is a critical assumption, because it links the collection of raw material to the overall use of territories. It means that the places in which people obtained raw stone were also the places where they routinely hunted and gathered.

In studying the stone artifacts from Bandelier National Monument, I found that the raw materials people selected changed somewhat over time and space. Because specific sources of these materials can be identified, the changes reveal variations in the places the Pajaritans traveled to and from during hunting and gathering expeditions. Indeed, from stone tools we can get rough estimates of the distances people traveled from any given village and of the relative size of the surrounding territory a village claimed. This last observation, I think, ultimately

Figure 8.4. Simple, expediently made stone tools.

Figure 8.5. Raw materials. Left to right (back): obsidian and basalt; (front): chert and heat-treated chert.

including the aptly named Obsidian Ridge, the slopes of Rabbit Mountain, and the peaks surrounding the Valles Caldera. Basalt—by far the most common stone in these parts—appears in its greatest abundance (and highest quality) near the mouths of Ancho and Lummis Canyons, along the Rio Grande, and generally over the southeastern reaches of the plateau. Chert gravels eroding in the northeastern sector of the plateau, notably at canyon mouths stretching from Guaje Canyon in the south to Garcia Canyon in the north, probably originated around Cerro Pedernal.

As many as 95 percent of all flaked stone tools in Bandelier National Monument were made from one of these three materials. Each is of a good quality for forming sharp, durable implements. Each is abundant and accessible right on the Pajarito Plateau. And significantly, each is more or less geographically exclusive of the others, appearing in local outcroppings in different places. If we examine the amount of each raw material the Pajaritans used for tool manufacture at any one village, we can get a notion of how often those villagers traveled to various parts of the plateau. Generous amounts of chert, for example, strongly imply a concentration of hunting and gathering in the plateau's northeastern quarter.

Apparently these three principal raw materials were not equally preferred for all tool types. Some 70 to 80 percent of all arrowheads for the entire Pajarito Plateau were flaked from obsidian. But for all other tools, villagers had their own preferences for local raw materials. This pattern is particularly evident in the cases of basalt and chert. For example, among all cutting and scraping tools from the main portion of Bandelier National Monument, basalt tools outnumber those made from chert by

provides a clue to a prehistoric boundary that likely was recognized by the ancestors of present-day Keres and Tewa people.

Raw Stone

Pajaritans used three primary types of stone to fashion their flaked stone tools: obsidian, basalt, and chert. Each of these rocks looks distinctive, and significantly, each is limited in its natural distribution across the Pajarito Plateau. Sources of obsidian are generally confined to the northwestern plateau,

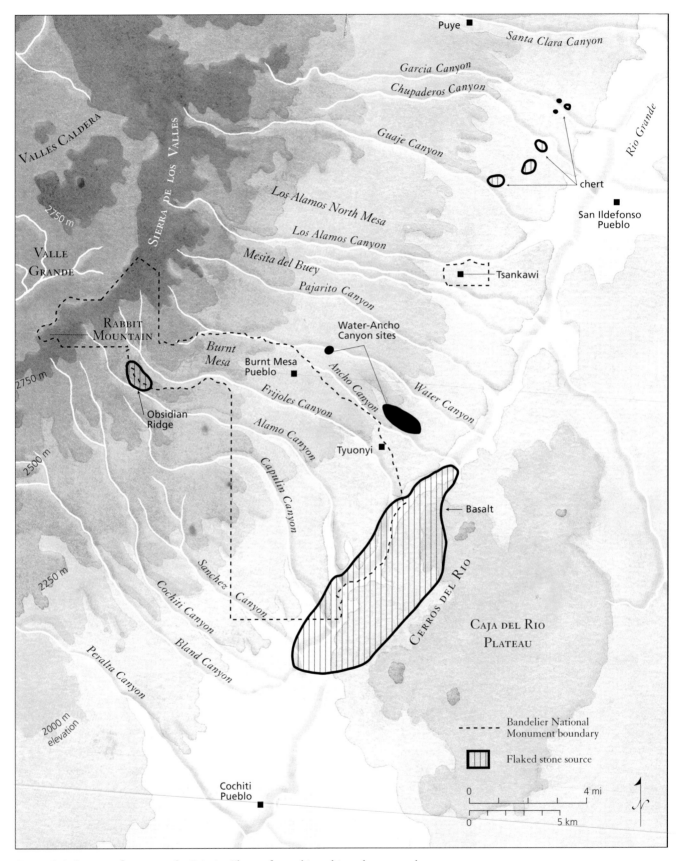

Figure 8.6. Sources of stone on the Pajarito Plateau for making chipped stone tools.

approximately eight to one. Contrast this with figures for the Tsankawi area, just six miles to the northeast, where cutting and scraping tools made of chert outnumber those of basalt by more than ten to one. In terms of basalt and chert, then, the inhabitants of the two places appear to have held precisely opposite preferences.

Why select one material over another? I think the inescapable answer is simply that local materials prevail. Pajaritans living within the main unit of present-day Bandelier chose local basalt to the near exclusion of chert, whereas residents of Tsankawi exploited nearby chert sources to the near exclusion of basalt. This overall pattern of conspicuous preference for local materials is recognized by archaeologists the world over; we call it the "distance decay model." The model simply states that the quantity of a material at an archaeological site will decline in direct proportion to the site's distance from the source of the material. On the Pajarito Plateau, obsidian appears not to follow this pattern as strictly as either chert or basalt, but the exception holds only for arrowheads. Far fewer obsidian cutting and scraping tools than arrow points were found at Tsankawi, which lies somewhat farther from Obsidian Ridge, than in main-unit Bandelier. Not surprisingly, far more obsidian cutting tools were found in Bandelier proper, which is much closer to the source.

The distance decay model would easily explain the varying proportions of basalt and chert in different parts of the plateau were it not for two nettlesome observations. First, the general pattern of distance decay is in fact violated in one small area near the eastern margin of Bandelier, as I discuss later. Second, the actual percentages of the two raw materials appear to have been affected over time by some unknown factor. For example, the proportions of basalt tools from sites near Tsankawi—never very high—began to decline even further at about 1250, until, by the 1300s, basalt tools were almost entirely supplanted by tools made of local chert. Conversely, in Bandelier, chert tools—again, never abundant—began to decrease around the same time. These shifts cannot be explained by changing technology; the types of tools used over time remained identical, and only the raw materials

changed. Nor does the distance decay model explain why, if people were able to acquire some stone from a relatively distant source at one time, they later could obtain virtually none of it.

To solve this puzzle, it is important to recognize two factors besides simple linear distance that affected a group's access to a source of stone. First, distances to rock sources should be measured not only as the crow flies. Physical barriers such as steep-walled canyons present challenges that cannot be gauged in mere miles. A simple glance from the visitor's center in Frijoles Canyon illustrates how daunting a "mere" mile can be if it includes scaling a cliff face or two. Second, social barriers might have existed that discouraged travel to and from certain quarries. People might not have been forbidden to cross social boundaries or forcefully constrained from doing so, but they were at least discouraged either by habit or through unfamiliarity with "foreign" terrain. The Pajaritans surely must have thought about social barriers—as real as any cliff face—and so we should think about them today.

Social Boundaries on the Pajarito Plateau

Between 1250 and 1300 Pajaritan tool makers increasingly used local raw materials, as we see in rising percentages of basalt at Bandelier main-unit sites and increasing percentages of chert in pueblos around Tsankawi. Because archaeologists have assumed that the gathering of raw stone was embedded in people's other tasks, this trend suggests that Pajaritans were now venturing less far from home and therefore that the sizes of the territories available to individual pueblos were diminishing.

Because these territories provided wild plant and animal foods, perhaps one of two other things was going on as well. First, farmers might have been producing more crops, leading people to gather fewer wild foods and use ever-smaller territories. Yet we see no corresponding decrease in the actual numbers of tools thought to have been used in preparing wild foods—just a steady change in the materials from which the tools were made. The second, and favored, explanation is that people were competing more over wild resources and began to place a premium on recognizing, respecting, and even guarding territorial borders. The trend toward greater use of local stone played out during the same years, 1290 to 1325, in which the human population of the larger Pajarito Plateau reached a peak. In the face of increased competition over land—or, more accurately, for the wild resources on it—the Pajaritans might have arrived at the notion of "trespassing."

The apparent trend toward territoriality leads us to think about what we might call "social distance," in contrast to geographical distance. One thing that might have inhibited travel on the Pajarito was prohibition of trespassing on a neighbor's territory, which would have increased the practical distance to a source of stone. That is, a quarry situated close by but in a territory that another group defended against trespassing was, in effect, just as difficult to use as one located a great distance away. In contrast, a quarry lying relatively far away but freely accessible might seem "nearby." I think it likely that increased social distance developed on the Pajarito Plateau along with notions of territory. Both likely were consequences of increased competition for land by an ever-expanding population.

I mentioned earlier that the overall pattern of distance decay fails to hold in one small part of the plateau—the mesa tops between Frijoles, Ancho, and Water Canyons on the eastern edge of Bandelier National Monument. According to the model, we ought to see that people in this area preferred basalt, because it clearly was the closest, easiest stone to obtain. Instead, when I studied the stone tools from eleven villages overlooking Ancho and Water Canyons, I found something unexpected. The artifacts from only one of the eleven pueblos showed that its inhabitants had overwhelmingly preferred basalt. In another four sites, villagers appeared to have relied strongly but far from exclusively on basalt. At one site, tool makers overwhelmingly favored chert, and in an additional three pueblos they used chert for a slim majority of stone tools. At two sites they appeared to have favored basalt and chert about equally. A mixed and curious result indeed.

At six of eleven sites in this area, then, people paid no attention to their physical distance from

stone sources, at a time when Pajaritans elsewhere on the plateau were increasingly looking for the nearest source of raw material. The distance decay model cannot explain these mixed results, but the social distance model can. The modern descendants of the Pajaritans themselves verify this explanation.

In the early twentieth century, John P. Harrington, a noted anthropologist and linguist, visited the Pajarito Plateau to document geographical terms used by the modern Tewa Indians. Besides collecting the place-names of important ancestral sites and geographical features, Harrington inquired about the traditional border separating the Tewas in the north from the Keres in the south. The boundary, he learned, was reckoned somewhere between Ancho and Frijoles Canyons, perhaps on present-day Burnt Mesa, a prominent tableland that separates the two canyons. A significant site on this mesa—Burnt Mesa Pueblo—has been closely examined by archaeologists (see chapter 15). Here is what they found in the stone tool inventory.

In the earlier portion of the site, inhabited between 1230 and 1275, basalt dominated chert by a little more than five tools to one. Clearly the inhabitants preferred basalt, and considering the village's location near basalt outcrops, this is precisely what the distance decay model predicts. For the later portions of the site, however—first occupied a little before 1290—the researchers found a surprising shift in raw materials. Basalt and chert tools now appeared in roughly equal numbers, with a very slight advantage to basalt. In other words, the proportion of chert rose dramatically, at the expense of basalt, even though neither the pueblo nor the stone sources moved. How are we to account for people's apparently increased preference for chert from the distant northern reaches of the plateau? Might it mean the villagers were discouraged from using nearby basalt quarries? Or encouraged to use northern sources of chert?

Returning to the eleven sites in the Ancho Canyon area, I suggest that they represent small Tewa and Keres groups who coexisted at around 1250. As they tested and ultimately defined new territorial boundaries, they left behind a mixed record of northern and southern ties. Burnt Mesa Pueblo, a single site viewed over a longer time span, may represent one social group whose affiliation was Tewa all along. Its blood tie became significant, however, only after a Tewa-Keres boundary was finally established around 1290, just to the south of the village. If I am right, then the boundary Harrington was told about has remained unchanged for more than seven hundred years—something no country in the modern world can claim.

I am not suggesting that either the Tewas or the Keres themselves symbolized their ethnic identity through their preference for a type of stone. I emphatically do not want to read more into the choice of chert or basalt than is warranted. But what we observe is unexplained by physical distances to stone sources or by changes in technology. I do think an explanation lies in the idea of social distance. The Tewa and Keres people, in their own histories, separate themselves north and south. And in the archaeological record a pattern on and around Burnt Mesa suggests a similar north-south line of separation.

Archaeologists attribute patterns in the archaeological record to nebulous concepts such as "ethnicity" with great reluctance. We trouble ourselves mightily over the very definition of the term, and we do not draw such borders lightly. In this case, however, we benefit from two converging sources of information. First, the people whose ancestors once lived on the plateau recognize a historical ethnic boundary at a specific place on the plateau. Second, we find at this very place an unexpected deviation from a time-tested model used in archaeology. This is a coincidence we cannot ignore. It is tempting to suggest that one can, sometimes, get blood—and ethnic groups—out of stones.

Michael R. Walsh was a member of the Pajarito Archaeological Research Project and is a research associate of the Cotsen Institute of Archaeology at the University of California at Los Angeles.

Figure 9.1. Archaeologist Judy Miles sorting sherds from the surface of a pueblo site.

From Broken Pots to Shifting Boundaries

James M. Vint

Our crew hiked over the juniper-covered mesa on yet another transect near the mouth of Lummis Canyon in Bandelier National Monument. We had been surveying all morning. I took off my pack to get a drink of water and, looking down, discovered that I was standing on a small field house—a single masonry room with a handful of scattered Agua Fria Glaze-on-red potsherds and not many more obsidian and basalt flakes. Since it was close to noon, we decided to break for lunch there. As we sat amid our packs munching sandwiches, our talk shifted to the usual archaeological anecdotes and hyperbole about previous field seasons and memorable finds.

Our crew chief, Judy Miles, quickly became the target of several stories involving the more exciting discoveries of the survey. Judy was legendary for finding the cool stuff—whole pots, hafted axes—objects rarely found on survey. Two field seasons earlier, while recording a field house not much different from the one where we now sat eating lunch, Judy was flagging artifacts to mark the site limits. A low ridge of tuff bedrock near the field house formed a natural boundary nearby. The tuff was scarred with small ledges and overhangs better suited for hiding snakes and lizards than pottery, so you can imagine the general surprise when Judy calmly announced that she had found a whole Espinoso Glaze Polychrome bowl (see plate 16). It had been stored and forgotten in a small overhang nearly six hundred years earlier.

Now, sitting there munching a dry granola bar, I tried to come up with my most exciting find and instead ended up feeling like Charlie Brown on Halloween: "All I got was a handful of Agua Fria Glaze-on-red sherds." But in archaeology, potsherds are as important as whole pots, if not more so. Like most other archaeologists, I get a thrill out of finding the cool stuff. But the discovery of sherds or even whole pots isn't the end of the archaeological process. Pots are much more than objects. Because they were made and used by people in a living society, they can tell us about many aspects of that society, such as trade, social identity, and the ways social practices and economies changed over time. In the Southwest, where sherds are often the most common artifacts found on sites, pottery is a cornucopia of information.

What can we learn from pottery? Clays and paints can be chemically analyzed to discover where a pot was made. A vessel's style and method of manufacture can often tell who made it, when, and where. And the changing decorative styles of pottery are used to date sites.

Sherds are such excellent clues precisely because they are both common and numerous. The simple field house where we ate lunch was once a farming outpost used by a family who recognized themselves as members of their pueblo community—a social group distinct from communities on the other side of Frijoles Canyon. For Charlie Browns like me, the exciting thing about archaeology is not the occasional whole pot but the chance to reconstruct intangible things such as social and economic relationships from simple artifacts like a handful of sherds.

Figure 9.2. Examples of culinary ware vessels.

Pajaritan Pottery, Trade, and Specialization

For the Puebloans who lived on the Parajito Plateau between 1150 and 1600 CE, pottery was the container of choice for storing, preparing, cooking, and serving food. People used baskets, too, but as they began to dry and store more food such as corn, beans, and jerked meat, they must have found pottery more efficient for the prolonged soaking, boiling, and stewing needed to make dried foods edible. Families owned a variety of unpainted cooking jars made with a gray-firing paste and either a smooth or a corrugated surface, the latter created by pinching the coils of paste from which the vessel was built. Archaeologists call this type of pottery "culinary ware."

The shapes and sizes of culinary ware pots were somewhat determined by their utilitarian purposes. Even the pinched coil decoration was functional: the corrugated surface served as a "radiator," transferring heat away from the pot and helping to prevent it from cracking as it heated and cooled by

Potters' Materials

Paste is a mixture of clay and tempering material—sand, crushed rock, or crushed potsherds—that potters add to strengthen the clay. Chemical analysis of the clay and petrographic analysis of the temper in ancient pottery can help identify the geological and geographical sources of the raw materials, which can then be linked to the communities where the vessels were made. The mineral paint used on black-on-white pottery typically contained manganese or iron to create the black color. Glaze paint, which was introduced to the northern Rio Grande region in the early 1300s, contained lead or copper that became glassy when vessels were fired. Early glaze paint tended to be a strong glossy black, but over time the lead content of the paint increased, resulting in very runny paint.

Figure 9.3. Santa Fe Black-on-white bowl.

enabling the clay to expand and contract.

Puebloan painted pottery was more varied in form and decoration than was culinary ware. People typically used painted vessels not for cooking but for storing and serving food. Vessels included bowls, jars, pitchers, ladles, seed jars, and canteens, as well as miniatures and effigy forms. The Pajaritans used ollas to haul and store water, and bowls to serve meals. They kept prepared food, seed for planting, and other perishable items in sealed jars to deter rodents, insects, and moisture.

From about 1000 to 1325 CE, Puebloans throughout the northern Rio Grande region made vessels decorated with black paint applied on a white background. Over time, potters invented new technologies and decorative styles. By the early 1300s they were decorating pots with red, white, or yellow backgrounds and lead-based glaze paint. This is the renowned "glaze ware" of the Classic period. Potters from the southern Pajarito Plateau, including Bandelier National Monument, to places south

of modern Albuquerque made glaze-painted pottery and traded it up and down the Rio Grande Valley. We even find some as far east as Kansas and as far west as the San Pedro Valley of southeastern Arizona.

Interestingly, glaze ware is scarce north of Frijoles Canyon, where Pajaritans continued to make black-on-white pottery. The post-1300 types there are called "biscuit ware," because their soft, porous paste resembles the initial bisque, or "biscuit," stage in the firing of modern porcelain. Later, I return to what it means that potters on the southern Pajarito Plateau shifted from black-on-white to glaze-painted pottery while those on the northern plateau stuck with black-on-white ware.

Before about 1300, black-on-white pottery, principally a type called Santa Fe Black-on-white, dominated the Pajaritans' decorated pottery. Analysis of Santa Fe Black-on-white paste suggests that potters made this type everywhere it is now found. Even so, people in neighboring communities traded it to one another (it probably wasn't exchanged over long distances). We see no major differences in the way Puebloans made or used Santa Fe Black-on-white pottery throughout its geographical range of manufacture, and no evidence that trade barriers existed between regions. From 1100 to the mid-1200s, Puebloan communities appear, at least from an economic perspective, to have been relatively independent, and their residents traded with people in nearby communities who made a living more or less the same way they themselves did.

It may seem strange that pottery manufactured in virtually every pueblo was also traded, but in economies where exchange is carried out by barter, trade is only one part of a complex economic and social relationship. Equally important are gift giving and the feeding and lodging of trade partners and their relatives. Such trade relationships, which may span generations, establish and maintain long-term obligations between partners. These long-standing reciprocal relationships allow partners to rely on each other for food or other goods in times of need, even if immediate reciprocation is impossible. Gifts of Santa Fe Black-on-white pottery between Pajaritan trading partners might have been one means of banking future assistance.

The plateau-wide distribution of Santa Fe Black-on-white ended in the early 1300s, coinciding with the founding of large villages such as San Miguel, Yapashi, Tyuonyi, and Tsankawi and the introduction of glaze-painted pottery. Initially the new pottery appeared only in the southernmost portions of Bandelier, but it gradually spread northward. During the 1400s, potters across the plateau began to specialize in the manufacture and trade of glaze and biscuit ware vessels. This specialization soon became an important part of the economy in the northern Rio Grande Valley and on the Pajarito Plateau. As population grew and large pueblos developed, villages became both increasingly interdependent and competitive. This may seem like a contradiction, but by now, depletion of resources such as wood and game meant that community interdependence became paramount. As drought gradually worsened, some Puebloan families adopted new ways of supplementing their household and village food supplies. By specializing in the produc-

tion of certain goods or services, families and communities could trade with others to obtain food and reduce their day-to-day dependence on farming, hunting, and gathering.

A good example of such specialization took place at Tonque Pueblo, now an archaeological site near modern San Felipe Pueblo, where potters became intensive producers of glaze-painted pottery in the late 1400s. Vessels made at Tonque are found on the southern Pajarito Plateau and throughout the northern Rio Grande. They show the importance of ceramic manufacture in Tonque's economy as well as the social and economic links created through trade between villages.

The importance of economic relationships among Pueblo people was highlighted in a study by Richard Ford, an archaeologist. Historically, members of different Tewa pueblos specialized in certain goods or services. Ford noticed that San Juan Pueblo was known for the blankets and baskets its artisans made. Santa Clara Pueblo was recognized for rattles and other ritual items, and both villages were famed for their superb pottery. San Ildefonso was noted for its potters' decorated wares, and Nambé for cooking pots. Midwives from Tesuque and San Juan aided surrounding communities. Although we have too little evidence from the Pajarito Plateau to identify goods produced in individual pueblos, we do have evidence to suggest that Pajaritans produced and traded glaze-painted pottery, perhaps as specialists in the larger sphere of exchange.

Do Pots Equal People?
When I am asked how we can identify groups of people through archaeological data, I jokingly say, "Some people made red pots and some people made white pots." Although this is a goofy simplification, a link did exist between pots and the people who made and used them, and it can be measured archaeologically. One of the first to explore this idea in New Mexico was Harry P. Mera, a medical doctor and self-taught archaeologist. He proposed in 1935 that decorated pottery styles could be tied to groups who spoke different languages. After scrutinizing the pottery at the many Pueblo sites he visited during his far-ranging fieldwork in the northern Rio Grande,

Figure 9.4. Biscuit ware bowls and jar.

Mera suggested that glaze-painted pottery was made primarily by ancestral Keresan and southern Tanoan speakers and that black-on-white and biscuit wares were made by ancestral Tewa people. He based his hypothesis on the observation that glaze-painted vessels predominated around Albuquerque, in the Galisteo Basin, and on the southern Pajarito Plateau, where the Keres live or are known to have lived. Black-on-white and biscuit pottery, in contrast, predominated from the northern Pajarito Plateau northward through the Espanola Valley to the Taos region, areas long home to Tewas.

Mera's idea gained further support in an early-twentieth-century study carried out by the anthropologist John P. Harrington. Tewa people explained to Harrington that both they and the Keres recognized the land between Frijoles and Ancho Canyons as the boundary between their traditional territories.

Whether or not common but distinctive objects such as pots truly represent language or ethnic groups remains vigorously debated. Although it seems logical that people who produced and exchanged vessels of the same style participated in the same economic and social networks, they need not necessarily have belonged to the same ethnic or language group.

We have long known that during the Coalition period (1150–1325 CE), Santa Fe Black-on-white

was the most abundant decorated pottery type, appearing with smaller amounts of Kwahe'e Black-on-white. Around 1325, people living on the southern Pajarito Plateau began making and using glaze-painted pottery, notably Agua Fria Glaze-on-red, the earliest in a series of glaze wares that continued to be made until the 1600s. This pottery first appeared at the southern end of present-day Bandelier National Monument near San Miguel Pueblo. As people who made and used glaze-painted pottery founded and settled new villages, the ware spread north and eastward, reaching the vicinity of Yapashi around 1375 or 1400.

For at least a time, deep, sheer-walled Alamo Canyon, just east of Yapashi, marked the northern limit of glaze-painted pottery. Around 1400, people in Frijoles Canyon, north of Alamo, began to use glaze-painted vessels. From that time through the mid- to late 1500s, people continued to use a variety of glaze-on-yellow and glaze polychrome ceramics in Frijoles Canyon and villages to the south. North of Frijoles and Ancho Canyons, biscuit ware types (which succeeded Santa Fe Black-on-white) continued to be made and used—for example, at Tsankawi and other large pueblos on the northern Pajarito Plateau. We rarely find glaze-painted pottery in substantial quantities in this region.

During the 1400s and 1500s, the terrain between Frijoles Canyon and Tsankawi may have

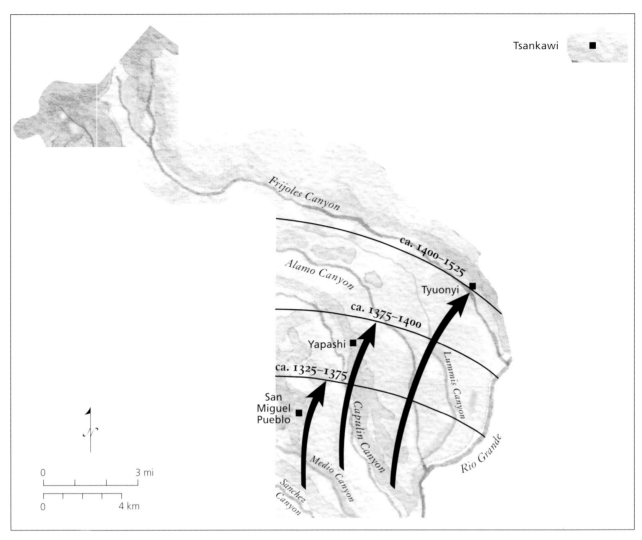

Figure 9.5. The spread of glaze ware vessels across what is now Bandelier National Monument.

been something of a no-man's land separating the heavily settled southern and northern parts of the Pajarito Plateau. This buffer might have helped reduce direct competition between the villages over resources. The many deep canyons and narrow mesa tops in this area also served as physical boundaries between communities. Altogether, the boundary between people with glaze ware and those with biscuit ware traditions developed and moved rapidly northward across the Pajarito over the course of seventy-five years. By the late 1400s it reached the area that Harrington had been told was a boundary between the Keres and Tewa peoples.

Does this northward movement of glaze-painted ware reflect the expansion of ancestral Keres populations, as Mera proposed, with people migrating northward over time? Or does the movement of the boundary mirror the changing nature of trade networks rather than ethnic or linguistic differences? I am inclined to argue for a bit of both. The adoption, development, and use of technologies such as a particular way of making pottery become culturally ingrained, and over time the pottery style may become a signature of a cultural group or region, just as architecture or clothing can be. It was not without reason that Dorothy, upon landing in Oz, exclaimed, "We're not in Kansas any more!"

Reconciling Conflicting Evidence

Although glaze and biscuit pottery give us tantalizing clues about the geographical dimensions of pottery trade and social boundaries, we must also look at other archaeological evidence to see whether it supports or contradicts our findings. For example, do the archaeological distributions of types of stone used in tool making support a Frijoles Canyon boundary?

In chapter 8, Michael Walsh identifies a boundary immediately north of Frijoles Canyon, perhaps in the vicinity of Burnt Mesa Pueblo. There, stone tool makers used primarily basalt before about 1290 but much greater proportions of chert after that date. Walsh attributed this shift to the establishment of a territorial boundary that made acquisition of basalt, which outcropped south of the boundary, more difficult for residents of pueblos north of the boundary. As we have seen, the pottery evidence indicates such a boundary only at about 1400.

Why the difference in timing? I believe the likely explanation is that people procured and produced pottery and chipped stone tools under different economic and social circumstances and exchanged them over different networks. Territorial claims that made it difficult for people to obtain certain kinds of stone became established before traders introduced glaze pottery into the area, and stone apparently was not widely traded. Ceramics, in contrast—especially glaze-painted wares—were exchanged across territorial lines. Why? Perhaps because decorated pottery is much more "visible" in social situations than is raw stone. Puebloans used decorated pottery to serve food during public and ritual events as well as at home. Such visibility subtly conveys social information: who traded with whom, which communities maintained regular contacts with each other, and what a group's social status was. In other words, pottery held social meanings beyond its practical uses, and those meanings may have been different from the meanings of stone tools.

Although we are far from completely understanding the complex web of economic and social networks the Pajaritans created, we can piece together clues by studying handfuls of sherds and chips of stone from simple field houses. Big pictures are composed of humble pieces, and the Agua Fria sherds we found at a nameless, 650-year-old farmstead are small but important fragments of the social history of the Pajarito Plateau.

James M. Vint was a member of the Bandelier Archaeological Survey and is an archaeologist with the Center for Desert Archeology in Tucson, Arizona.

Figure 10.1. Stairs on the mesa north of Garcia Canyon.

Ancient Trails of the Pajarito Plateau

James E. Snead

In the late 1890s the former governor of the Territory of New Mexico, LeBaron Bradford Prince, made a long-anticipated pack trip into the wilds of the Pajarito Plateau west of Santa Fe. In addition to being a political heavyweight, Prince was an avid student of the region's pre-Columbian inhabitants; a dusty collection of relics added flair to his fashionably Victorian home. On this occasion Prince's excursion took him into what is now Bandelier National Monument to visit the Shrine of the Stone Lions, described nearly twenty years earlier by Adolph Bandelier. In the process, Prince found himself musing over another of the plateau's secrets, one about which Bandelier had said little. Ancient trails, worn deeply into the bedrock, led to and from villages abandoned before the Spaniards ever arrived in the Southwest. "They are not 'footprints on the sands of time,'" Prince wrote in a small book published after his journey, "but in the rocks of eternity."

In the 1980s and 1990s I was part of the archaeological teams from the National Park Service that comprehensively studied Bandelier National Monument, and we, too, used the old trails. Looking for a way to climb a difficult canyon slope, we sometimes hiked around an outcrop to spy a smooth set of steps leading upward, a path built in ancient times by Puebloans facing the same problem. We were following, quite literally, in their footsteps.

Ironically, until recently we knew almost as little about these trails as Prince did. For generations, researchers working on the Pajarito Plateau concentrated on its residential pueblos as sources of information about the past. Digs at these sites yielded the traditional items of archaeological interest: pottery, stone tools, wooden beams for dating, and plant and animal remains pertaining to diet and farming. Trails, in contrast, seemed to offer little useful information.

In recent years we have begun to pay attention to a picture bigger than that painted by our excavations. Because people of an earlier era spent most of their time outside their homes, the argument goes, shouldn't we be searching for evidence of what they did outdoors? And shouldn't we use this information to develop new interpretations of past lives? Embracing such an approach, we can see the archaeological record not as simply a matter of disconnected "sites" where things can be dug up but as the combined traces of a whole cultural landscape— a place where topography, environment, and the countless, subtle features left behind by human action can be viewed together as a complex record of human history.

The isolated canyons of Bandelier offer an extraordinary proving ground for the cultural landscape approach. Visible but little noticed under the piñons and ponderosa pines are the fields the ancestral Pueblo people used, the small shelters they built to keep out of summer storms, the lookouts they maintained to watch for game and visitors from other villages, and the petroglyphs they placed to convey information to knowledgeable observers. Knitting this landscape together, giving it structure and meaning, is the faint but tangible network of ancient trails. In other parts of the Southwest, particularly at Chaco Canyon, archaeologists have

Figure 10.2. Ancestral Pueblo trail at Tsankawi, photographed in the early twentieth century.

Figure 10.3. Parallel paths worn into the tuff bedrock west of Tsankawi Pueblo.

identified a network of roads that was important to local society. Trails, if somewhat less dramatic, clearly played similar roles.

To explore this idea of cultural landscape, some colleagues and I launched the Pajarito Trails Project in the early 1990s. Building from a foundation laid in earlier research, I developed a standard recording procedure for trails and set out to look for them in Bandelier and other parts of the plateau. The vast scale of the region and the modest resources available meant that we set no deadline for completing the project; we do the work as time permits. Yet with the support of the National Park Service, the Friends of Bandelier, and Los Alamos National Laboratories, we have already compiled a fascinating body of information about the Pajarito trails.

Trail Structure

Interpreting the Pajarito trails involves, first, the deceptively simple process of documenting their characteristics. It seems simple because the volcanic geology of the Pajarito Plateau creates unique conditions for trail preservation. The same soft, tuff bedrock that allowed the ancient inhabitants to carve rooms into the sheer canyon walls can be eroded by the passage of human feet, meaning that the oldest trails are quite literally worn into the stone. Centuries of foot traffic have marked these routes deeply and unmistakably. In some places, two or even three separate trails run parallel to each other or are interwoven. Many of these trails show signs of having been constructed intentionally, with steps and other features carved into the rock by hand.

Figure 10.4. Petroglyph trail marker to the right of stairs at Tsankawi.

Despite these advantages, determining the age of a trail can be a problem. In many places, trails made yesterday might look identical to those made centuries ago. I once spent an entire morning working with a field crew of the Bandelier Archeological Survey recording a trail marked by cairns of piled stones, only at last to meet the hiking stockbroker who was setting them up. True ancestral Pueblo trails, however, usually include features lacking in more recent examples. The Puebloans' concept of steps, for instance, was quite different from ours. Instead of wide, flat, American-style steps, theirs were the width of a single foot, and the climber negotiated them as if on a ladder. Most impressive are the elaborate sets of steps known as staircases, which often extend for dozens of feet up the steep canyon sides.

Particular trails are also marked by petroglyphs. We find these trail markers in various situations, but usually they appear on rock faces where people climbing up from below could easily have seen them. One trail near Tsankawi ascends the cliff face immediately next to a dramatic petroglyph of a male figure that clearly marks the route. Other trail markers also consist of humanlike figures and geometric designs. Although we don't understand the symbolic repertoire of the trail markers, it is tempting to see them as indicators of territory or perhaps local identity that people traveling through would have readily understood.

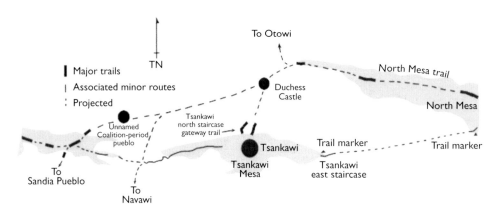

Figure 10.5. Route of the North Mesa Trail through the Tsankawi area.

The Trail System

So far my colleagues and I have recorded more than seven miles of trails on the Pajarito Plateau. This figure sums only the combined lengths of visible trail "segments" that we have observed and is thus a fraction even of those that are already known. Entire swaths of the Pajarito, particularly to the north, have never been surveyed for trails, and we think it likely that the original system stretched for hundreds of miles. Even with this small sample, we are increasingly able to understand the organization of the trails as they snake across the landscape.

With the available evidence we divided the Pajarito trails into three categories: local trails, major trails, and trail networks. Local trails appear to have been used only by people who lived in their immediate vicinity. They were routes leading from mesa-top farms to sources of water in the canyons below, or paths to small hilltop shrines. Major trails linked people and places separated by greater distances, ultimately forming a system that spanned the entire Pajarito and connected it to surrounding regions. In some cases major trails can be still be followed for miles. In others they are visible only when they cross a topographic obstacle such as a narrow, rocky ridge, where they are sometimes worn more than three feet deep. One trail in particular, the Old Pajarito Trail, may originally have run the entire length of the plateau, linking northern communities near Puye to those in the vicinity of Cochiti, dozens of miles to the south, and passing through many of the most thickly settled tracts en route.

Trail networks are more complex yet. They consist of trails or trail segments positioned so close together that they cannot really be considered separately. A trail network is most evident at Tsankawi, where we found seventy-four segments on a single mesa. The Tsankawi trails are bewilderingly complicated, linking the community house on the mesa top with cavate pueblos and other features on the flanks of the mesa and all of them to the valley below. This network was created by centuries of changing patterns of movement, a process ongoing even now. Some of the ancestral Pueblo trails at Tsankawi are part of the interpretive loop established by the National Park Service and show signs of recent wear, whereas adjacent segments that are not part of the system are disused and covered by pine duff.

Many of the major trails connect pueblo sites that date to the beginning of substantial ancestral Pueblo occupation of the plateau, probably before 1200 CE. These trails run east-west, from the Rio Grande to the Jemez Mountains, and north-south, traversing canyons to connect small settlements. Interestingly, people seem to have used these trails even after they abandoned their small settlements in favor of larger, later pueblos, which often lay some distance from the main routes. The North Mesa Trail, for instance, links several of the older sites, is deeply worn, and includes several constructed stairs. Although Tsankawi Pueblo lies directly south of this trail, most of the feeder routes that connect it to the major trail are relatively modest. The simplest explanation for this pattern is that the North Mesa Trail was established during the initial colonization of the plateau and continued in use even after many of the places it originally connected had been abandoned.

It is also apparent that the trail network saw use long after most Pajaritans had moved down into villages along the Rio Grande. During the historic era, the Pajarito served as a hunting ground, sacred retreat, and refuge for the Pueblos, who used the trails to travel across the mesas as their ancestors had before them. In several places major trails are blocked by game traps—deep pits hacked into the bedrock to be used in hunting deer. Such traps would have been both inconvenient and dangerous at a time when the trails were used every day. The deer population must have been lower then, too, especially in residential areas. The game traps likely were made in more recent centuries, when deer were the only permanent residents of the plateau.

Guard Pueblos

As we gain a better understanding of the movement of people along the Pajarito trails, we begin to find answers to other archaeological questions. For instance, they may help us to better understand the way in which local communities were organized. In the historic period throughout the Southwest it was important to pay close attention to people traveling along trails, to keep an eye on both friend and foe. In some cases people built "guard pueblos" as watchposts from which to monitor traffic and protect the home village. The modern Hopi-Tewa community of Hano, in Arizona, began as just such a guard pueblo three hundred years ago.

The way several of the smaller Pajarito pueblos relate to the trail system suggests that they might have served as guard pueblos. A good example is a pueblo called Duchess Castle that sits in the valley north of Tsankawi Mesa. Duchess Castle is situated near the point where the North Mesa Trail would have crossed the valley from east to west. It also lies on the most logical route between Tsankawi and the Otowi community to the northwest. Because the flat valley bottom in the vicinity offers many good places for building a pueblo, the position of the site at the probable intersection of these trails is not just a coincidence. It is reasonable to imagine the residents of Duchess Castle guarding the junction on behalf of their kin on the mesa top to the south. Rainbow House in Frijoles Canyon is another good candidate for a guard pueblo, and there may well be others.

Gateway Trails

We often notice during our surveys that some of the Pajarito trails are far more complicated than was necessary to make travel easier. Sometimes the Pajaritans laboriously carved steps into relatively gentle slopes or established a parallel route even though an older route appears to have been quite adequate. I am increasingly convinced that the action of constructing the trail was as important as the trail itself and that the process was deeply symbolic.

The clearest example of this sort of labor investment comes from the half-dozen staircases recently recorded on the plateau. Each one has deeply incised steps, additional features such as handholds, and parallel and sometimes intertwined routes. In the Capulin Staircase in the southern part of Bandelier, several intertwining sets of stairs, each composed of dozens of steps, climb the face of the steep slope of Capulin Canyon. When taken in context with associated trail markers, this complex represents a remarkable effort when in fact just one of the parallel routes would have sufficed.

I suggest that the making of these elaborate staircases was an activity important in its own right. In Pueblo ritual, repetition is part of what makes an act sacred. Repeated cycles of song, dance, and prayer reaffirm relationships between people and the cosmos and serve as constant reminders of those ties. Some physical tasks, such as plastering the interior walls of ceremonial rooms and kivas, appear to be parts of repetitive rituals as well. Some ancestral Pueblo kivas excavated by archaeologists show evidence of continual replastering. One, at the village of Hawikuh, near Zuni, was replastered at least sixty-three times, and a kiva in Frijoles Canyon shows evidence of twenty replasterings. It appears that the plastering and repainting "renewed" the walls and the images on them, perhaps demonstrating the piety of those who took part. It seems possible that building other features had a similar purpose. Perhaps the periodic renewal of trails and stairs was a ritual act rather than merely construction to improve traffic flow.

energy into stairs rather than gates, but they were responding to a similar impulse. Anyone coming up the trail from outside the community would have turned a corner and seen a magnificent stairway ahead, a sign of the spiritual propriety and strength of the people who lived there. I call these features gateway trails. Together with trail markers and nearby guard pueblos, they served notice to travelers from the outside that they were approaching a place with a strong history and identity whose people were to be treated with caution and respect.

Trails and "Human Space"

The ancestral Pueblo trails of the Pajarito Plateau yield a surprising amount of information about the activities of the people who used them. They represent patterns of movement at different scales that literally tell us who went where and when. Putting that information together with other knowledge about the cultural landscape, we can reconstruct economic strategies and political organization. Above all, the trails indicate that networks of travel across the Pajarito were established early in the human history of the region and remained in use until very recent times. As we survey new areas we will better understand the nature and extent of the system.

Figure 10.6. Tsankawi North Staircase, a gateway trail to Tsankawi Pueblo.

It is also interesting that only certain sets of stairs were treated in this way, and usually no more than one per community. I think this reflects something akin to the building of entryways into medieval European towns: there were many ways in and out, but only one formal "gate" for important ceremonies and processions. Ancestral Pueblo people put their

I also think it is evident that trails were not simply functional. Ancestral Pueblo people went everywhere on foot, and the evidence suggests that their movement itself had symbolic connotations. Over time, as people walked the same paths to and from their villages, shrines, fields, neighbors, and hunting grounds, the routes took on a sacred character. Trails leading to Tsankawi, Yapashi, Puye, and Tyuonyi were invested with meaning that would have been of potent significance to those who walked along them. Periodically the people built stairways to make that meaning clear.

All of this suggests that the archaeological study of trails is important for understanding how the Puebloans organized their world—how they created "human space" from nature. As the Pajarito Trails Project continues, we will get a firmer grasp on the network of movement and interaction across the plateau. Perhaps the best summary of the potential that the trails offer to our understanding of the Pajarito Plateau comes from Bradford Prince, who wrote that they "tell vividly and more lastingly of the long occupation and vast numbers of people of those ancient ruins than could the most enduring monument."

James E. Snead was a member of the Bandelier Archaeological Survey and is an assistant professor in the Department of Sociology and Anthropology at George Mason University.

Figure 11.1. Kenneth Chapman and Eleanor Johnson tracing cavate pictographs in 1915.

Carved in the Cliffs
The Cavate Pueblos of Frijoles Canyon

Angelyn Bass Rivera

Peering into one of the hundreds of cave dwellings carved deeply into the cliffs on the eastern flank of the Jemez Mountains, visitors try to imagine the lives of the Puebloans who built and lived in them centuries ago. We can all appreciate the hours of labor people put into creating them, speculate on the tools they used to carve them, marvel at the images they painted on the walls and ceilings, and imagine generation upon generation of householders weaving cloth, making pottery, and grinding corn.

Though archaeologists have studied the "cavates" for more than a century, we still do not know exactly why and how they were built or used. Cavate pueblos display most of the features of the large, free-standing masonry pueblos and were clearly used as residences—but why did Puebloans build dwellings in the cliffs when it might have been easier to build stone-walled pueblos in the open? The presence of cavates becomes even more curious when, as in Frijoles Canyon, they are situated next to masonry pueblos where people lived at the same time.

More than a thousand cavate rooms dot the walls of Frijoles Canyon, and countless more nestle in the cliffs of the Pajarito Plateau. Cavates and their interior features give us a rare glimpse into the daily lives of Puebloans of earlier times. Cavates were dwellings of the ancestors of modern Pueblo people who still make their homes in the Rio Grande Valley. The Tewa word for cave dwelling is *t'ová tewha*, which also translates roughly as "old or crumbling village against the wall."

The cavates that honeycomb the sheer tuff cliffs of the Pajarito Plateau are unique in the Puebloan architecture of the American Southwest. Not only are they excavated out of rock (hence the name cavate), but their interiors hold beautifully preserved features that people used for food preparation, storage, and weaving. Some cavates have painted and incised plaster and petroglyphs that hint at formal ceremonial use.

Today the cavate pueblos appear as a multitude of partial and complete chambers. Originally, some reached four stories high and encompassed both cavates and exterior rooms that were built partly or entirely of stone masonry. Little is left now of the exterior masonry rooms, which collapsed long ago. At Long House in Frijoles Canyon, for example, all that remains of the exterior portions of this once large cavate pueblo are stone foundations at the base of the cliff, plastered areas on the cliff face that were once the back walls of rooms, and horizontal rows of empty sockets that once held roof beams.

Just down canyon from Long House, at Talus House, many cavates are fronted by the remains of exterior masonry rooms. To help visitors imagine what the now-collapsed walls once looked like, Talus House includes a reconstruction built in the early part of the twentieth century by Kenneth Chapman, an anthropologist, and a Tewa Indian crew from San Ildefonso Pueblo. They built Talus House on original masonry foundations uncovered by Edgar Lee Hewett, the first archaeologist to conduct extensive excavations in Frijoles Canyon.

From these past excavations, as well as more recent surveys and studies of the cavates, we know that Puebloans began constructing cavate pueblos

Figure 11.2. Cavates along the north cliff face of Frijoles Canyon.

in the mid-1200s CE. They continued building them until the mid-1500s, with a peak in use in the 1400s. We calculated this chronology from different sources: analysis of pottery found inside the cavates and on nearby talus slopes, tree-ring dating of wood excavated from cavates, and archaeomagnetic dating of a few hearths. In Frijoles Canyon, the dates reveal that the cavates were occupied at the same time as the masonry pueblo of Tyuonyi, though we are still unsure of the exact relationship between the cavates and the large, freestanding pueblos. The chronology of cavates in other parts of the Pajarito Plateau is less well known than that of Frijoles Canyon, but most cavates were probably built during the drought-punctuated 1400s and early 1500s. As in Frijoles Canyon, the other cavate villages lie close to large, Classic-period masonry villages and permanent sources of water.

Cavate Construction

Cavates of the Pajarito Plateau were carved into layers of volcanic ash known as Bandelier Tuff. These layers formed during two separate eruptions and ash flows from the Valles Caldera volcano, the first approximately 1.6 million years ago and the second about 1.2 million years ago. Portions of the tuff are weakly cemented, especially at the junction of the two ash flows. Puebloans took advantage of this weakness by excavating cavates where the flows met. To get afternoon sunlight during the cold plateau winters, they cut caves into south- or south-east-facing cliffs. North-facing cliffs and canyon bottoms, in contrast, are shaded in winter by mid-afternoon. From the deep striations and gouges in most of the cavate ceilings, we can tell that their builders pecked, carved, and chiseled out the soft tuff with tools such as digging sticks and sharpened stones, cutting progressively deeper into the cliff-face bedrock until the room reached a desired shape and size.

Most cavates are single chambers, but some are connected by doorways. The Puebloans occasionally built masonry walls and partitions inside the cave rooms, as well as front walls and entrances to rooms

Figure 11.3. An intact partition wall of a cavate.

After carving a cavate, many builders intentionally sooted its interior. The soot not only created a uniform interior color and texture but also hardened and coated the grainy tuff surface to prevent it from crumbling. After blackening the ceiling and walls, people scraped the soot off the lower half of the walls (to provide a solid bonding surface) and then plastered that portion and the floor. Cavate plaster was composed of clay, silt, and sand and often included organic matter such as grass to help it cohere.

Plaster served several purposes. As a protective coating, it shielded the tuff from water. It also insulated the room, controlled dust, and provided a smooth finish for painted or incised designs. Cavate dwellers finished their floors, too, with earth plaster, creating a hard, smooth surface on which to sit, sleep, and work at mealing bins, hearths, and looms. Often the wall plaster is an extension of the floor plaster, indicating that builders created floor and wall surfaces at the same time.

Most cavates have an interior dado, or band of plaster covering the lower half of the walls. This plaster band measures approximately one and a half to three feet high—about eye level if one is sitting on the floor. Above the dado, the wall is sooted tuff. On rare occasions, cavate residents fully plastered the room's interior, including the ceiling. Some cavates have many layers of plaster (one has more than thirty), revealing that people frequently refinished their rooms. When they replastered the dado, they often started the new layer slightly lower on the wall, leaving a dark band of the older plaster exposed at the top. Frequently, residents decorated this dark band with incised images. A few rooms have figures or geometric designs painted on the walls, and some have petroglyphs carved into the sooted walls and ceilings.

Since at least the 1200s Puebloan people have

cut in the rock. Unfortunately, because of exposure to the elements, only a few examples of such masonry remain in place today. Most have collapsed, leaving just a trace of building material behind as a clue.

The shapes and sizes of the cavates vary considerably. Most are semicircular, but some are rectangular. The builders usually made the ceilings hemispherical rather than flat, almost certainly because they knew this shape provided structural stability in the soft tuff. In the same way an arch or an egg has tremendous strength because of its curved shape, cavates with hemispherical ceilings can withstand the weight of the rock above, making them less likely to cave in. Though some cavates have collapsed, this appears to have been due to rock falls and centuries of weathering and erosion.

Figure 11.4. The interior of a large cavate with dado, sooted tuff, and petroglyphs.

plastered the walls of rooms and painted portions of kivas with murals. At Bandelier, the plastered walls of some cavates display wall paintings. Snake Kiva, excavated by Hewett in 1909, is so called because a large horned serpent, or Awanyu, is painted along the curving back wall. In the 1930s, fragments of this painted surface plaster flaked away to reveal another mural beneath it: an anthropomorphic head, in profile, with a feather headdress, painted in red, yellow, and white. Several other exposed patches of yellow and red paint along the wall suggest that this earlier mural extends all the way around the cavate. Such layered murals are suggestive of other complex narrative murals found at Pueblo sites such as Awatovi, Pottery Mound, and Kuaua. The murals at these villages were painted for specific ceremonies and plastered over at the completion of each one. Perhaps the Snake Kiva mural was covered for the same reason.

The Use of Cavates

We cannot say exactly how cavates were used, because their functions might have changed over time, but we have many clues. In the 1980s, the archaeologist H. Wolcott Toll identified three broad categories of cavate rooms: habitation rooms, storage rooms, and special-purpose rooms. He based this classification on two important characteristics: a cavate's size and the kinds of features found inside and around it. By now archaeologists have examined more than a thousand cavates in Frijoles Canyon, and more than three quarters of them proved to be living rooms with areas of 25 to 90 square feet. Fewer than a quarter consist of smaller storage rooms, measuring between 3 and 22 square feet. Least common are the much larger special-purpose rooms, many of which, such as Snake Kiva, appear to have been used for ceremonies. Only thirteen special-purpose rooms have been recognized among the Frijoles Canyon cavates, ranging in size from 83 to 189 square feet.

Cavate living rooms contain features that tell us much about their inhabitants' activities. Builders often paired plastered or stone-lined hearths or fire boxes with cylindrical smoke holes or vents for air circulation. Many rooms contain plastered recesses

Figure 11.5. Snake Kiva. The broad zigzagging band is the horned serpent's body; his head is on the left.

Figure 11.6. Metates and mealing bins in a Bandelier cavate. Note the scuff marks left on the wall by grinders' feet.

Floor ridges, which are unique to cavates, are mounded seams of adobe running across a room, separating lower and higher floor sections (see plate 20). Because the hearth and mealing bins tend to be grouped on the same side of the ridge, it may have divided the room into work and sleeping or storage areas. Earthen metate rests and mealing bins, used for grinding corn, are other built-in features.

Loom anchors offer one of the most interesting clues to the use of some cavates. The only traces left of weavers' looms are large sockets in cavate ceilings and rows of small wooden loops set deeply into the floors. The ceiling sockets held wooden hooks from which the upper bar of a vertical loom was suspended, and the weaver tied the lower bar to the wooden loops. Loom anchors appear in both habitation cavates and special-purpose ones but are rare in masonry pueblos such as Tyuonyi (though this may be a result of poor reporting by early archaeologists). When we find weaving features in the large pueblos, they usually are in kivas. In the cavates, both loom anchors and mealing bins generally appear in second-story or even higher cavate rooms. The upper-level cavates may

and niches carved into the walls and floors in various shapes and sizes for storing pots and other household items. Careful examination of the ceilings and walls reveals many sockets and holes of different sizes. Some of the large sockets held wooden supports for looms or perhaps upright beams. Smaller holes might have held long, narrow wood rods or sticks on which people hung clothing and blankets.

have been good places in which to work, because many of them opened to the outdoors and had natural light. Interior rooms in masonry pueblos and cavates are very dark, and it is difficult to imagine anyone grinding corn or weaving cloth in such a small space by firelight. Indeed, people probably carried out many of their daily tasks on the roofs of the masonry rooms fronting the cavates.

Figure 11.7. Cross section of a cavate room positioned high on a cliff face.

Figure 11.8. A storage cavate containing a clay *puki*, an implement used as a base in molding pottery.

Storage rooms were the second most common type of cavate chamber in Frijoles Canyon. Archaeologists call them storage units because they have few or none of the interior features used in daily living. They tend to be smaller than cavate living rooms, too, and they are often sooted but not plastered. A few are finished with a plaster dado, which might mean that their function changed over time, from habitation to storage or vice versa. Storage chambers vary in size from large niches in the walls to individual rooms. Some storage rooms sit high on the cliff face, reachable only by hand-and-toe holds or by ladder from the roofs of nearby rooms. A few storage cavates in Frijoles Canyon still contain prehistoric corncobs. We assume that stockpiling food for the future was essential, and these small, featureless cavates served ideally for such use.

The rare special-purpose cavates, larger than living rooms, tended to have a greater number and variety of interior features such as hearths and loom anchors in the floors, as well as painted and incised plaster. Edgar Hewett called these cavates "kivas," but Adolph Bandelier's Cochiti guides insisted during his visit to Frijoles Canyon in 1880 that the cavates were houses. They pointed out that the kivas were in the valley below.

Were these cavates kivas? Unlike most kivas, the cavates are not subterranean and have no distinct *sipapu*, or spirit hole, in the floor. Though large by cavate standards, they are much smaller than kivas found in contemporaneous large pueblos (see chapter 6). On the other hand, most of these chambers sit physically separate from other cavates, which gives them a certain prominence. Like Snake Kiva, they all have wall paintings and incised images in their interiors. Kenneth Chapman, who studied the incised images in Frijoles Canyon cavates, thought these rooms had ceremonial importance because of their paintings of birds, snakes, humanlike figures, and geometric designs, which in Pueblo culture are usually associated with ceremonial practices. The art historian J. J. Brody points out that except for decorated pottery, most kinds of Pueblo art made before 1900 were created as components of rituals. For these reasons it seems likely that the thirteen largest cavates were used in part for religious activities, although the rituals performed in them might have differed in important ways from those conducted in other, larger kivas.

With a summary in hand of what is known about cavates, we can return to the question raised at the beginning of the chapter: Why did Puebloans build dwellings in the cliffs? Perhaps the answer is simple: It was, for the most part, easier and more practical to carve and shape cavates than it was to build freestanding masonry pueblos. So far as we can tell, the soft volcanic tuff was fairly straightforward to carve. This made it relatively easy to tailor spaces for dwelling, storage, or special use and might have required the use of fewer resources such as mud mortar and shaped stones. Furthermore, the rock provides natural insulation in all seasons.

It is clear by now that the cavates were built and used at the same time as the large, freestanding masonry pueblos, but the question remains, How did the two differ? One of the oldest and most compelling arguments is that people used the cavates seasonally, primarily in the winter, but lived in the large pueblos year-round. Those who argue for winter use point to the journals of Adolph Bandelier, who wrote that his companion from Santa Clara Pueblo described the cavates as winter habitations. The presence of small ceremonial rooms and the absence of large kivas suggest indoor, possibly winter ceremonies held by a small number of participants, in contrast to large public ceremonies performed in kivas and plazas during warm summer weather.

Alternatively, the well-insulated cavates stay cool in the summer heat, which makes them practical summer residences as well. The presence of loom anchors and mealing bins in second- and third-story cavate rooms that open to the exterior may mean that weaving and grinding meal were occupations in the summer, too. After spending several summers working inside the cavates and noticing how cool they are, I am convinced they were used year-round. Nonetheless, the question of how and why the cavates were used is far from settled. Very likely, archaeologists will still be debating their purpose many years from now.

The Cavates Live

By the mid-1500s, many of the people who lived in Frijoles Canyon cavates had moved to other pueblos and places closer to the Rio Grande. The cavates remained uninhabited for nearly a century until the Pueblo Revolt of 1680–1692, when once again a few became homes for Puebloans seeking refuge from the Spanish. Though Pueblo people no longer used the cavates after 1700, the dwellings remain alive in modern Pueblo memory, perception, and tradition. Pueblo people still visit them and acknowledge them as an integral part of an ancient landscape to which they are strongly connected.

For the rest of us, cavates are fascinating. They are unique both because of their construction and special features and because they illuminate the lives of former inhabitants. It is the cavates that capture in their architectural details the daily activities of grinding corn and weaving fabric. It is the cavates, rather than the freestanding pueblos such as Tyuonyi, in which the details of ancestral Puebloans' domestic lives are still visible. Archaeologists will continue to study the evidence and grapple with the issues of the cavates' origins and uses; others will be content to peer into the interiors and marvel at what they see.

Angelyn Bass Rivera is an archaeological site conservator at Bandelier National Monument.

Figure 12.1. Hanat Kotyiti.

Plate 13. Snow in Frijoles Canyon.

Plate 14. Storm on the Pajarito Plateau.

Plate 15. Flat panel of tuff covered with petroglyphs along an ancestral Pueblo trail near Tsankawi Pueblo.

Plate 16. Left: Agua Fria Glaze-on-red bowl; right: Espinoso Glaze Polychrome bowl. Both were found during the Bandelier Archaeological Survey.

Plate 17. Obsidian nodules and flakes at an ancestral Pueblo quarry near Rabbit Mountain.

Plate 18. Glaze ware bowls, a jar, and a donut-shaped scoop from the northern Rio Grande Valley.

Plate 19. Cavate rooms in Frijoles Canyon.

Plate 20. Interior of a large cavate room, showing a floor ridge possibly used to divide the room into work and sleeping or storage areas.

Plate 21. A cliff kiva on the eastern edge of Alamo Canyon.

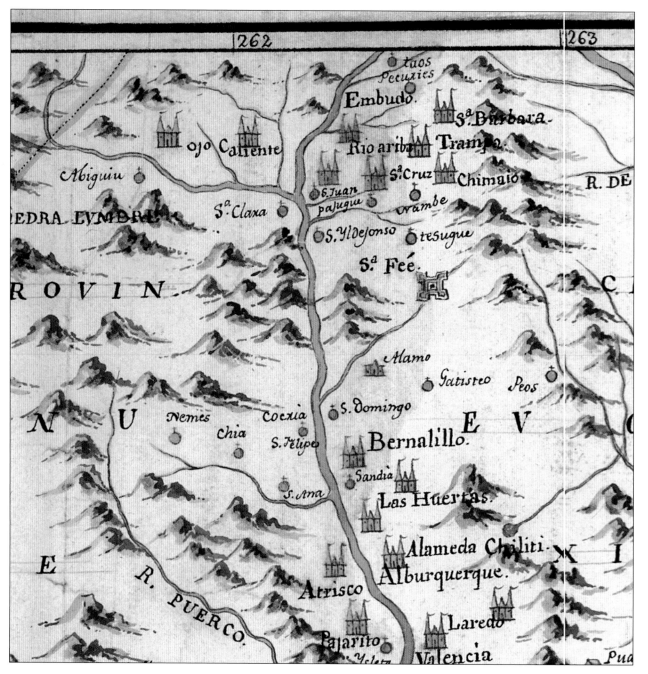

Plate 22. Detail of a map by José de Urrutia showing Spanish royal domains, 1769.

Plate 23. Yapashi Pueblo, also known as Village of the Stone Lions.

Plate 24. The Cerro Grande fire of 2001, a severe crown fire on the Pajarito Plateau.

The Journey from Shipap

Robert W. Preucel

It is through the oral tradition that their journey on the hiyaanith *(path of life)*
is told—the whole of their Pueblo culture's development and experience.
—Simon Ortiz, "What We See"

On October 8, 1880, Adolph Bandelier and Juan José Montoya of Cochiti Pueblo climbed the steep trail to the summit of Potrero Viejo, a narrow mesa just south of what is now Bandelier National Monument. There they found the old village known as Hanat Kotyiti ("Cochiti above") in a remarkable state of preservation. Bandelier wrote in his journal: "The ruins themselves, though large and well preserved, are still more barren than those of Pecos.… It is evident that the pueblo has been burnt, and Juan José says that after a long and unsuccessful blockade, the Spanish dragoons finally surprised the pueblo. They burnt the pueblo, thus compelling its people to abandon it." Bandelier was particularly interested in the site because it allowed him to test Cochiti oral historical accounts against his firsthand observations and Spanish documents. He wrote that "as in every other instance where I have compared the Spanish documents with the localities, and with current tales, I have found them to be of great accuracy, and in substantial agreement with the traditions of the people."

Bandelier's interest in Pueblo Indian oral history has not been widely embraced by Southwestern archaeologists. In the 1920s such well-known figures as Alfred V. Kidder and Frederick W. Hodge largely discounted oral history as a source of information because of its perceived biases. Perhaps because it was so dismissed, many scholars considered it unnecessary to consult with Puebloan people when writing their culture histories. In the 1960s the "new archaeology" replaced the culture history approach, emphasizing scientific methods and testing of hypotheses. Many of its proponents were critical of ethnographic analogy—the use of observed activities to understand the past. Archaeologists tended to describe Puebloan prehistory according to the idea that cultures were "adaptive systems" that changed in response to factors such as environmental change. With few exceptions, Pueblo people rarely found themselves consulted or involved in archaeological research.

Today, I and many other Southwestern archaeologists are reevaluating our standard methods and assumptions as we reconsider our relationships with contemporary Indian people. We increasingly appreciate the implications of different kinds of knowledge, from science and history to oral history. In part this change is due to the Native American Graves Protection and Repatriation Act of 1990, which has both required and encouraged archaeologists to work more closely with Native people and has fostered a new humanistic perspective in archaeological theory. Oral history plays a vital role in the collaborative research project I am currently conducting with the people of Cochiti Pueblo. It throws important light on the Cochiti people's migrations from the southern Pajarito Plateau to their current home along the Rio Grande.

Oral History and Archaeology

What is oral history? Simply stated, it consists of spoken accounts of the past that are at least a generation old. Traditional Puebloan societies have two broad kinds of oral history—secular and sacred. Secular oral history is stories told by grandparents to grandchildren, traditionally on cold winter evenings. These stories deal with fundamental kin relationships and include tales of marriage and abduction, tales of witchcraft, and coyote tales. Sacred oral history includes the accounts given to neophytes when they are initiated into religious societies. These usually tell of origins and migrations and include the story of the great flood and the genesis of plants, animals, and death. Both kinds of stories may refer to supernatural beings and to historical details such as names of ancestral villages.

Archaeologists have commonly held that science is superior to oral history, because, they argue, the data and methods of science are objective and open to public examination. But science does not really stand outside of society; its assumptions and practices are always rooted in culturally shaped beliefs. In Western society, knowledge is something to be widely shared, but in Pueblo communities it is shared carefully and selectively. When Pueblo people acquire sacred knowledge, they also acquire serious responsibilities for the proper use of that knowledge. Making sacred knowledge public may compromise ceremonies as well as the status of traditional religious leaders.

Oral history is both a kind of knowledge and a way of communicating that knowledge. Some elements of it may indeed be historical and can be verified, whereas other elements may be mythological, used to pass on moral principles and teach proper behavior. The challenge for archaeologists is to work with Indian communities to use oral history to its greatest effect to create more complete cultural narratives.

The Cochiti Migrations

For the past seven years the Pueblo of Cochiti and I have conducted archaeological research at Hanat Kotyiti, the village visited by Bandelier and Montoya. Together we are documenting the meaning and significance of this ancestral Cochiti village. Hanat Kotyiti was built and occupied during the Pueblo Revolt of 1680, a time when the Pueblo people lived free from Spanish rule. Part of our research involved gathering oral history, and we proceeded in two stages. First, we put together all previously published examples of oral history related to Hanat Kotyiti. Second, we interviewed Cochiti elders and recorded their accounts on videotape and audiotape. (These interviews were conducted with the understanding that they are the property of Cochiti Pueblo and are not to be published without authorization.)

In our literature review we found a surprisingly large number of stories dealing with Hanat Kotyiti, collected over the years by anthropologists, linguists, historians, photographers, and tourists. The earliest were gathered by Adolph Bandelier in the late nineteenth century. Charles Lummis, a Los Angeles journalist and sometime traveling companion of Bandelier's, wrote down a version of the same migration story. The linguist John Peabody Harrington gathered migration stories from Juan de Jesús Pancho (John Dixon) in 1908. Ruth Benedict recorded tales and stories in 1924, and the photographer Edward S. Curtis visited Cochiti briefly the following year and gathered several stories. Frank Applegate published the story "Lost Cochiti Gold" in 1932. Most recently, in 1997, the historian Marc Simmons published a version of this account.

In 1999 Mars Chalan and I interviewed three elders who shared with us their traditional stories of Hanat Kotyiti as well as about their personal experiences when visiting the village. As I listened to the elders, I soon realized that they did not regard their accounts as describing isolated historical events. Rather, they considered their stories part of a broader narrative tracing the movements of the Cochiti people from village to village, all the way back in time to the emergence of people from the underworld at a place known as Shipap. This view is well illustrated in a migration account titled "How the People Came Up from Frijoles," originally told to Ruth Benedict in 1924 by Santiago Quintana (Cyrus

Figure 12.2. Adelaido Montoya (right) and Adolph Bandelier in Frijoles Canyon.

Dixon), a member of the Cochiti tribal council, and published in her book *Tales of the Cochiti Indians:*

Long, long ago, when everything began to live again after the flood, the people came out in the north. It was when they left White House that they began to have trouble. The people lived together in Frijoles Canyon. They lived all together at the mesa of the Stone Lions: the people of Cochiti, of Santo Domingo, of San Felipe, Acoma and Laguna and the people of Sia. They all spoke the same language, and they lived as brothers. At last they had trouble. The headman of one people took his families in one direction, and another in another. The descendants of one mother went together with one headman. The people of Santo Domingo followed down the east bank of the Rio Grande till they came to Cactus village [five miles from Cochiti]. The people of Cochiti went to the old pueblo of San Miguel [seven or eight miles north of Cochiti on the west bank of the Rio Grande] having followed down the Capulin Canyon from the mesa of the Stone Lions. The

people of San Felipe and Laguna and Acoma followed down the Peralta Canyon toward the west and built the [ruined] pueblo of Peralta Canyon [six miles from Cochiti]. There were people of the Corn clan among them, and they went off by themselves and lived with the Utes and the Apaches. The people of Cochiti lived at San Miguel. At last they had trouble. They came to the Potrero Plateau [Plateau of the Buildings, nearer Cochiti]. There they lived many years. They made war on the different pueblos, and they all tried to drive the people of Cochiti from their plateau. While they were fighting, the Spaniards came from the south. The rest of the pueblos leagued with the Spaniards against the people of Cochiti. All these pueblos had already come down off their mesas and had been given lands by the Spaniards. Only the people of Cochiti were still on their mesa. There was only one trail up to the pueblo, and at the top the people had piled boulders. When any enemy came up the trail, they rolled down a boulder and killed him. The Spaniards could not bring

Figure 12.3. Santiago Quintana, 1925.

people went up and down a secret trail to the north side for their water. There was no path; they knew the way down the face of the mesa where there was nothing but rocks. The Spaniards thought of a plan. They captured a [Cochiti] Indian who had been living a long time in Jemez. They made preparations to kill him, but just as they were about to put him to death, they told him that if he would show them the trail the people used going up and down for water on the north side of the mesa, they would set him free. He promised he would take them up the trail. That night he waited at the Moon Trail [secret trail] and took the Spaniards and the men of the southern pueblos up the face of the cliff. There was no path; they climbed from rock to rock. In the morning the people woke on the mesa, and they saw that the whole north side of the mesa was filled with their enemies. They saw there was no hope of resistance, for the Spanish had guns. They surrendered. The Spanish brought them down off the mesa, the women carrying their babies. The Spanish put them across the river at Tipute to the east of the present site of Cochiti.

The first thing to note about the Quintana account is the way it interweaves mythological and historical references. The first village named is White House, a village that figures prominently in all recorded Keresan migration accounts. It was the primordial village occupied after the people emerged at Shipap. It was the place where humans and supernatural deities lived together in harmony and where traditional customs were established. It was also the place where the first troubles started. According to stories told at different Keresan pueblos, White House was where, alternatively, men began to mistreat women, children began to disrespect their elders, or the people began to neglect katsinas.

Several scholars have tried to link White House to a particular archaeological site or district: Charles Lummis suggested Tyuonyi, Florence Hawley Ellis thought it could be Mesa Verde, and Steve Lekson and Cathy Cameron favored Chaco Canyon. I believe it might be more useful, however, to think of White House not so much as a fixed place but

the people down from their mesa. They went to Santa Clara and to Tesuque and the far-off pueblos to get help against the people [of Cochiti]. They could do nothing against them. There were a thousand warriors among the people [of Cochiti] then: it was the largest of the pueblos. No one could hurt them on their mesa. Many of the people of Santa Domingo, San Felipe, Taos, San Juan, Santa Clara, Nambe, and even the people of Picuris and Apicu [Abiquiu?] were killed in great numbers. They fled, and the people [of Cochiti] chased them, piling great heaps of stones along their way, one stone for each enemy they had killed. These piles of stones still remain all the way to the river. When the people had chased them across the river they returned to their mesa. The Spaniards came against them again from the south, with all the pueblos. They laid siege to the mesa. The

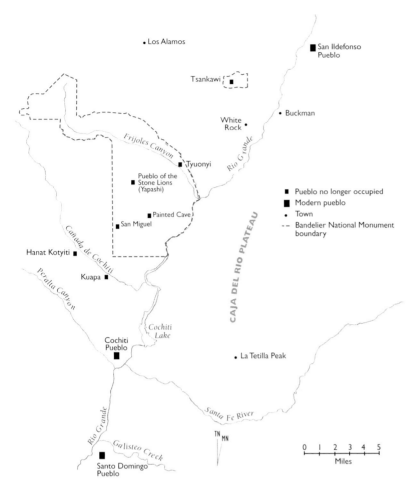

Figure 12.4. Villages mentioned in the Cochiti migration stories.

The following labels appear on the map:

Los Alamos

San Ildefonso Pueblo

Tsankawi

White Rock

Buckman

Frijoles Canyon

Tyuonyi

Rio Grande

Pueblo of the Stone Lions (Yapashi)

Painted Cave

San Miguel

Cañada de Cochiti

Hanat Kotyiti

Kuapa

Peralta Canyon

Cochiti Lake

CAJA DEL RIO PLATEAU

Cochiti Pueblo

La Tetilla Peak

Rio Grande

Santa Fe River

Galisteo Creek

Santo Domingo Pueblo

TN MN

■ Pueblo no longer occupied
■ Modern pueblo
• Town
-- Bandelier National Monument boundary

0 1 2 3 4 5
Miles

rather as an icon of a relationship to the past. I have argued that after the Pueblo Revolt of 1680, the pueblo of Hanat Kotyiti was likely built "in the image of White House." This was a time when Pueblo leaders were preaching a return to the "ways of the ancestors," and White House, as the original village, stood for exactly those ways and values.

The oral history also explains the origins of the different villages of Keresan-speaking Pueblos. It mentions undefined "troubles" in Frijoles Canyon that led to unrest in the community and caused different groups to leave. People moved, building a series of villages, and eventually established the modern pueblos of Cochiti, Santo Domingo, San Felipe, Zia, Laguna, and Acoma. Although Santa Ana, another Keresan pueblo, is not mentioned, the story clearly emphasizes the interrelatedness of all Keresan peoples and their beliefs.

The Quintana account contains historical

information, too. It mentions the siege of Hanat Kotyiti, which we know from Spanish documents took place on April 17, 1694. After fierce fighting, Diego de Vargas, governor of New Mexico, captured the village. Twenty-one warriors were killed, and 342 women, children, and old men were taken prisoner. The Spaniards seized nine hundred head of sheep and goats, some of which they recognized as having been taken in raids on Santa Fe. Four days later, the Pueblo warriors counterattacked and succeeded in freeing half the prisoners before withdrawing into the Jemez Mountains. Vargas then burned the village and its supplies and returned to Santa Fe. An interesting contradiction surfaces between the Spanish and Cochiti accounts. In his diary, Vargas claimed that he learned of the trails up the mesa from Bartolomé de Ojeda, a Zia ally. In Quintana's account, the Spaniards capture a Cochiti man living at Jemez Pueblo and torture him into divulging the trail location.

Several published versions of this narrative exist. One was told to Bandelier by José Hilario Montoya, a governor of Cochiti. It identifies the sequential occupation of Tyuonyi, the Pueblo of the Stone Lions, Painted Cave, San Miguel, Kuapa, Kotyiti, and the modern village of Cochiti. Montoya's account seems also to have been the basis for Charles Lummis's essay, "The Wanderings of Cochiti." A second version, given to Edgar Hewett by Juan de Jesús Pancho, mentions Tyuonyi, the Village of the Stone Lions, Painted Cave, San Miguel, Kuapa, Kotyiti, and Cochiti. John Peabody Harrington heard a slightly different version from Pancho in 1908. It identified the villages as Tyuonyi, the Pueblo of the Stone Lions, an unknown village, San Miguel, Kotyiti, and Cochiti. Comparing these accounts with those told at Cochiti today, what seems important is that certain sites are always mentioned, and the order in which they are named is always the same.

Figure 12.5. José Hilario Montoya at Yapashi, or Village of the Stone Lions, 1880.

Two of the villages, the Village of the Stone Lions and Kuapa, appear to have been especially closely related. The Village of the Stone Lions, also known as Yapashi, is a 350-room plaza pueblo with six kivas (see plate 23). Although we have no precise dates for it, archaeologists think the pueblo was occupied between 1290 and 1525 CE. A few hundred yards to the west of it lies the stone lions shrine, where two life-size, crouching mountain lions have been carved from the volcanic tuff. The Cochiti name for the village is "old village where the stone lions crouch." Bradford Prince referred to it as Pueblo Quemado because of its evidence for destruction by fire. This site and shrine hold considerable significance for many Pueblo people. Matilda Coxe Stevenson, an anthropologist who studied Zuni at the turn of the last century, noted that the Zunis regarded it as the entrance to the underworld and periodically made pilgrimages to it.

Kuapa, located in the Cañada de Cochiti, is the largest village on the Pajarito Plateau. It has at least twenty-one roomblocks and seven kivas. Test excavated by Nels Nelson in 1914, it is estimated to date from about 1325 to 1600 CE. Nearby are the ruins of Cañada, a historic Spanish village occupied into the nineteenth century. Bandelier wrote that "both the Indians of Cochiti and the inhabitants of Cañada, who are well versed in Indian folk-lore concerning their valley, have asserted to me that Kua-pa was an old village of the Cochiti tribe, from which they moved to the banks of Rio Grande where Cochiti stands today." He also noted that, according to Cochiti and San Felipe accounts, Kuapa was once captured by Tewas, causing people to take refuge for a short time on Potrero Viejo.

As Bandelier first observed, the Village of the Stone Lions and Kuapa share certain significant features that imply a common origin. Both are very large villages with multiple plazas and kivas, and both sit adjacent to a stone lions shrine. This pattern strongly suggests that an entire community moved south as an intact social unit and reproduced its sacred landscape, including its shrines, in a new context. The Pueblo of the Stone Lions is sometimes spoken of as the "mother village" and is extremely important to the Cochiti people.

The Rewards of Oral History
My collaboration with the Pueblo of Cochiti has been a richly rewarding experience. Through the patient guidance of Cochiti elders and with the help of Cochiti young people who worked with me as interns, I have come to understand aspects of the Pueblo past from a new perspective, one that emphasizes the continuity and interconnectedness of the past with the present. I have also learned the

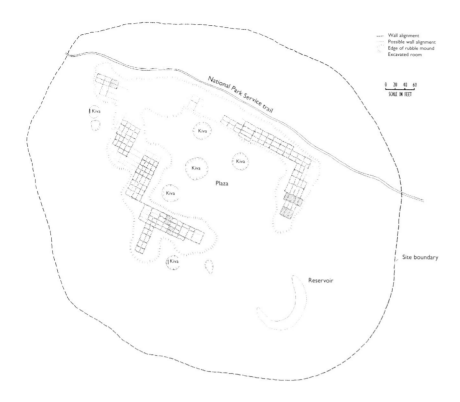

Figure 12.6. Plan of Yapashi.

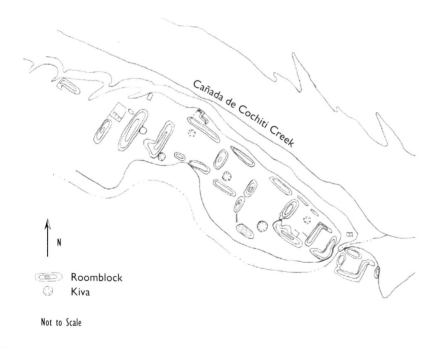

Roomblock
Kiva

Not to Scale

Figure 12.7. Plan of Kuapa, after a map made by the archaeologist Nels C. Nelson in 1914.

importance of oral history as a way of communicating cultural values and traditions. The villages of Tyuonyi, Pueblo of the Stone Lions, Painted Cave, San Miguel, Kuapa, and Hanat Kotyiti are alive with meaning for the Cochiti people. I feel strongly that archaeologists need to take a good look at oral history, as Bandelier did, in order to fashion more informed accounts of the past as it was and still is lived. For the people of Cochiti, as for those of other pueblos, oral history continues to ensure the continuity of their remarkable traditions and culture.

Robert W. Preucel, a former member of the Pajarito Archaeological Research Project, is an associate professor of anthropology at the University of Pennsylvania and the Gregory Annenberg Weingarten Associate Curator of North America at the University of Pennsylvania Museum of Archaeology and Anthropology.

Figure 13.1. Abbott's Ranch of the Ten Elders, with Tyuonyi in the foreground.

Writing History at Bandelier National Monument

Monica L. Smith

Our world today is reflected in documents: receipts, bills, letters, certificates, movie tickets, catalogs, newspapers. Our journey through life would quickly pile up to a huge volume of paper if we didn't sometimes go through it and discard what we no longer needed. But before the twentieth century, many lives went completely unrecorded, and little was written about even well-known persons. Whatever documents remain from those eras have become the texts of history. Fortunately, in the case of Bandelier National Monument, such fragments let us experience the region through the words of the first foreigners who came there.

Even if we mentally erase interstate highways, shopping malls, and Lottaburgers from the landscape, we find it hard to imagine the New Mexico seen by Francisco Vázquez de Coronado in 1540. Enticed by rumors of gold, he led the first expedition to the far northern reaches of what was then called New Spain, but his entourage met unexpected difficulties as it traveled beyond the known world. In a frank and plaintive letter he wrote: "The hardships have been so very great and the lack of food such that I do not believe this enterprise could have been completed before the end of this year, and even if it should be accomplished, it would be with a great loss of life."

Vázquez de Coronado found no gold, but rumors of wealth persisted, and later explorers were unde-terred by his experience. Spaniards established their first New Mexico settlement and capital in 1598 at San Gabriel de Yunque Owingeh, in the vicinity of today's San Juan Pueblo, but moved the capital to Santa Fe in 1610. For Spain, New Mexico lay always at the farthest edge of its colonial domain, as we can see in maps that end just north of Santa Fe. Trade and transport between the Rio Grande Valley and faraway Mexico City tenuously linked New Mexico with a European domain.

The American West sat on the fringes of colonial activity for decades. English and French colonists concentrated on the eastern portion of North America while Spaniards spread northward from their New World capital in Mexico City. These Europeans hungered for new knowledge, not only for scientific purposes but also for developing trade and extracting profitable resources. People recorded information about Spain's frontiers in logbooks, diaries, and letters to royal patrons, but the most visually stimulating display of new knowledge came in the form of maps.

Cartography in the sixteenth century must have been the equivalent of the computer revolution in our own era. The explosion of geographic discoveries, amplified with each new voyage, meant a constant revision of maps. Although Spaniards, fearing competition, hesitated to publish plans showing too much detail, other European map makers were

Figure 13.2. Large San Pablo Polychrome olla fragment from a historic-period rockshelter.

eager to fill in the gaps of information by producing new editions as fast as they could.

The presence of Pueblo peoples in what was to become northern New Mexico was known to map makers quite early. A map from 1570—fewer than eighty years after Columbus's first landfall—already shows the area of the Rio Grande and the Pajarito Plateau as the very edge of the explored world. Over time, increasingly detailed maps (see plate 22) revealed the landscape of the region and helped lure new generations of settlers. Into New Mexico came Spanish adventurers and religious leaders, Mexican householders, American traders and frontier settlers, railroad entrepreneurs, anthropologists and archaeologists, travelers and tourists, who together created a new American West.

Archaeology of the Earliest Encounters
When Spaniards came to New Mexico they brought with them not only a tradition of literacy but also new modes of life dependent on domestic animals such as horses and cows, foods such as wheat, and metal tools and armor. Householders and home-makers brought along their ideas of indispensable

goods: crucifixes, candles, amulets, and fancy Spanish pottery. Some of these could be re-created with local materials, but for others there was no substitute for the annual caravan of goods that lurched its way up the Camino Real (roughly parallel to the Rio Grande) from Mexico City.

Because few written records existed for northern New Mexico even in the Spanish era, archaeology is just as important for that time as for the centuries before the European encounter. The physical record of artifacts and architecture gives us a much broader picture of colonial life, allowing us to see the transformation of ordinary lives and the way in which new generations of inhabitants adapted to New Mexico's landscape and to each other. At Bandelier National Monument, physical remains of the past are especially important for understanding the historic period, a time when most Puebloans seem to have relocated to villages along the Rio Grande. In the canyons of the Pajarito we find occasional potsherds and cave paintings that show continuing use of the area, mostly by Puebloans but perhaps also by Spaniards and their descendants who had taken up native crafts such as pottery making.

The Pueblo Revolt of 1680 destroyed many Spanish documents in New Mexico, so archaeology is especially important for understanding the cultural traditions that developed during the first 150 years of Spanish colonization there. Archaeologists working at sites throughout New Mexico have documented how Spanish settlers adapted their culture to local circumstances, taking up new foods such as corn as a substitute for wheat and venison as a substitute for imported cattle, sheep, and goats. At the same time, Pueblo people welcomed animal husbandry into their farming lifestyle.

After Spain's reconquest of New Mexico in 1692, Spaniards' religious and civil authority over Pueblo people changed, but the way in which both groups made their living continued much the same. Traditional Pueblo lands were now formally allocated boundaries by the Spanish crown, and Spanish colonists officially requested land, too. The legal language of the time defined these land grants using natural features—trees, hills, arroyos, and other vague or transitory markers—to demarcate boundaries. The original 1742 grant of the land eventually known as the Ramon Vigil grant, parts of which later became Bandelier National Monument, was chartered on the basis of the following description: "Boundaries being on the north the lands which the Indians of San Ildefonse enjoy by right, on the south those of Captain Andrés Montoya, the Rio del Norte on the east, and the mountain range on the west." European settlers first claimed areas useful for agriculture, such as the broad floor of the Rio Grande Valley, as well as grasslands suitable for pasture.

For several generations after the reconquest, Spanish settlers remained few, their homesteads scattered up and down the Rio Grande. The census of 1750 showed only 250 families in Santa Fe, the largest European settlement in New Mexico at the time. Those few families could not have anticipated the coming transformations that would require their descendants to be more specific about boundaries, land rights, and accompanying water rights. Not much changed when Mexican independence released New Mexico from Spanish control in 1821, but the subsequent American occupation in 1846 brought a new and more exacting standard for legal boundaries—one that differed from both regional traditions and Spanish customs.

The Pajarito Plateau, best suited to the rain-fed agriculture of the prehistoric period, was one of the last places to be formally claimed and occupied by people of European ancestry in the late Spanish and early Mexican periods. By that time, the Bandelier area had become a zone where shepherds grazed their flocks, moving them among the pockets of grassland and camping in the cavate dwellings that had once sheltered Puebloan people. By the early 1700s a system of "sheep sharecropping" known as *partido* had developed throughout the region. Under this system, landowners and, later, storekeepers rented out their flocks in exchange for a guaranteed return of lambs and wool. After the owner's quota was met, the shepherd kept any excess wool or lambs.

Sheep production in northern New Mexico had some surprising consequences. The California gold-mining boom with its famous forty-niners sparked a sudden demand for provisions. New Mexico herders bred their animals to be sure-footed and sturdy, and hundreds of thousands of sheep walked to California as well as Colorado and northern Mexico before the development of the railroad. The demand for meat gave new impetus to ranching, and the resulting surge in grazing profoundly altered the Pajarito Plateau's ecological balance and helped shape the spare, open landscape that seems familiar and natural to us today.

The Railroad Era

With the arrival of the railroad in the 1880s, bulk goods could at last be hauled cheaply and quickly. The nearest line touched the Rio Grande at Buckman (see map 2), so the railroad's effects on the Bandelier area were indirect but considerable. Mining and logging settlements sprang up along the river and into the mountains. Loggers and miners used the railroad in a cycle of mutual dependence, because the railroad itself needed timber for bridges, trestles, and ties. Railroad developers turned a strategic eye to territorial claims and land grants, eager to take advantage of land allocations that worked in their favor.

Other livelihoods on the Pajarito Plateau, such as herding, continued throughout the railroad era.

Figure 13.3. Historic-period metal bell used by sheep-herders on the Pajarito Plateau.

Figure 13.4. A cavate with stovepipe used by sheepherders.

We know shepherds used the Bandelier area because of the artifacts they left behind and the inscriptions they etched in the cavates. Herders' modest resources are seen in the small debris of the working world—sheep bells and tin cans modified into buckets, for example. Using the ancient Pueblo trails, herders appear to have crossed to the Pajarito from Cochiti and Española, the places most often mentioned in graffiti found in the cavates of central Bandelier.

The boom and bust of the new towns around Bandelier was typical of other parts of the American West as well. The mining center of Bland, for instance, grew from nothing to a population of three thousand in six years. After a few years of success, the town just as quickly vanished. Some miners enjoyed a high standard of living when times were good; photographs show them dining on oysters brought in by rail in seaweed-packed barrels.

Yet archaeological finds suggest that the prosperity brought by the railroad was not available to everyone. The people who made the greatest use of the Pajarito Plateau were rough-hewn shepherds,

hunters, miners, and ranchers who made their living on the edges of the flourishing regional economy. Although historical documents emphasize the lavish wealth gained during boom times, our finds from Bandelier—tobacco and baking powder packed in sturdy tins; ammunition for hunting and warding off predators—paint a different picture. These most basic goods show that local prosperity was elusive. Shepherds and ranch hands, indebted to the company store and making a living under harsh conditions, enjoyed few possessions. We find no traces of the little luxuries that had become commonplace in nearby Santa Fe.

The Twentieth Century
By the early 1900s the Western landscape was becoming better known in the eastern United States, enticing further immigration. Maps became more detailed and contained the kinds of information, such as the locations of roads and water sources,

Figure 13.5. Historic artifacts collected during the Bandelier survey: glass bottles, hole-in-top meat can, tobacco tin.

required by a gentler breed of newcomer. Photographs, museum exhibits, and popular novels added to the public image of a romantic West. After many years without permanent settlements in what was soon to become Bandelier National Monument, in 1907 and 1908 Judge A. J. Abbott established the Ranch of the Ten Elders on the banks of Frijoles Creek. He grew fruit trees and built ditches across the narrow valley to irrigate some thirty acres of land. Early photographs show his fields reaching the very edges of the ancient pueblo site of Tyuonyi.

Throughout northern New Mexico, claims to land began to be based increasingly not only on its capacity for herding or agriculture but also on its natural beauty and archaeological remains. Archaeologists, as their avocation developed into a scientific discipline, brought additional attention to the leavings of ancient people at sites such as Tsankawi and Tyuonyi and prompted the first systematic investigations into the precolonial past. Local civic

leaders used archaeology, including the substantial archaeological remains in Frijoles Canyon, to strengthen sentiments for statehood.

By the early part of the twentieth century, flush with success at the creation of America's first federal antiquities act, Edgar L. Hewett and leaders of a variety of interest groups, including the people of Santa Clara Pueblo, proposed a large-scale Pajarito Park that would encompass not only what is today Bandelier National Monument but also much of the Pajarito Plateau. This ambitious proposal failed, but the smaller Bandelier National Monument was created in 1916. Initially managed by the U.S. Forest Service, Bandelier was turned over to the National Park Service in 1932. Early efforts to manage the park left their own archaeological traces. Loops of barbed wire found far into the backcountry testify to the earliest attempts to fence out herders and reclaim a parklike wilderness.

As the study of humans and their objects,

Figure 13.6. Sheep crossing Buckman Bridge across the Rio Grande, 1922.

archaeology tells the story of recent people as well as that of the most ancient inhabitants of the region. Trash from the early twentieth century, including fancy bottled beverages and car parts, displays the increasing affluence of visitors. Among the new settlers in the region were Vera von Blumenthal and her companion, Rose Dougan, the eccentric pair who constructed a house out of the blocks of a small pueblo ruin near Tsankawi. Their residence, known as Duchess Castle, was an art colony from 1918 to 1928.

More recent events, too, have left their marks on Bandelier National Monument. The Great Depression and the work relief programs developed by the U.S. government coincided with the growth of land-management agencies such as the National Park Service. One of the relief programs, the Civilian Conservation Corps, maintained a camp in Frijoles Canyon for seven years while workers built what are now the permanent park buildings in the bottom of the canyon.

The CCC camp was intentionally demolished at the end of the construction project, and its exact location was forgotten until archaeologists rediscovered it during the Bandelier Archeological Survey in the 1980s. We know from CCC documents that the Corps was formed to promote a trade and a wage for otherwise unemployed young men (no women were admitted). Camp life was designed to ensure strong morals and good conduct. Archaeological finds suggest that camp life didn't always "go by the book": the surveyors recorded 1930s beer cans and other alcohol containers at the camp, along with a perfume bottle that suggested something about the enrollees' contacts with the outside world.

During World War II, the ultra-secret Manhattan Project brought the country's top nuclear scientists to the remote Pajarito settlement of Los Alamos. Deliberately isolated from the rest of the world by the need for secrecy, the project's families had few recreational opportunities outside

Los Alamos. Like many visitors before them, they found a haven in the beautiful canyons of Bandelier National Monument. In many ways Bandelier in the twentieth century can be seen as a microcosm of northern New Mexico history—it was a place where national interests were served amid stunning scenery and compelling archaeological finds.

History in the Western sense begins when the first written documents make a record of human activities, but it doesn't end when those documents reach a conclusion. The routine actions of daily life contribute to the archaeological record through artifacts and the traces of architecture. The story of all of Bandelier's residents, whether native or newcomer, is told by what they left behind.

Monica L. Smith was a member of the Bandelier Archaeological Survey and is an assistant professor in the Department of Anthropology at the University of California, Los Angeles.

Figure 14.1. Edgar Lee Hewett, 1909. Signed, "To my old Friend Weyima Governor of San Ildefonso Pueblo. Edgar L. Hewett."

The *Frijoles Gazette,* Archaeology, and the Public on the Pajarito Plateau

James E. Snead

Visitors to Bandelier National Monument who leave the interpretive center and head up the trail quickly find themselves entering an ancestral Pueblo world. They walk past excavated kivas and reconstructed pueblo walls, peer into chambers, and climb ladders leading to dwellings cut high in the cliff face. Those reading pamphlets or taking rangers' tours learn further details about the lives of the people who built these places hundreds of years ago. Some perhaps ask questions about how researchers have come to know these things, but archaeologists themselves are not usually part of the story.

Yet there are many other stories that could be told along the Rito de los Frijoles, and some of them *do* concern archaeologists. Long before the interpretive trails were built, even before the creation of the monument itself, archaeologists came here and used the narrow valley as a testing ground for new concepts and practices. It is fair to say that events in Frijoles Canyon in the early decades of the twentieth century played a central role in the establishment of American archaeology.

Although this story may not be part of the conscious experience of visitors to Bandelier today, it underlies everything they see as they walk the trails. One part of the story concerns the teaching of new generations of archaeologists. Archaeology has always been a field discipline, a study of the past in which the hands-on experience of finding artifacts

in the ground is deemed essential. This accent on fieldwork has distinguished archaeologists from historians for a long time, but the process by which younger scholars gain such knowledge and skills has not always been obvious. The modern idea of the "field school," a setting for formal training in archaeological techniques, was to a considerable extent developed in Bandelier nearly a century ago.

Archaeologists working at Bandelier, besides preparing young professionals, emphasized public education. Knowledge about the past was not simply a scientific matter, they believed, but relevant to the interests of the greater populace. Equally important was the idea that learning about such history works best in the places where the discoveries are made—out of doors, often far from towns and modern conveniences. Practices that we now take for granted—creating a site museum, partially reconstructing ruins, even giving "campfire talks"— emerged from early Pajarito archaeology.

A final idea from the early days at Bandelier concerns the importance of the "past" that was on display there—that of the ancestral Pueblo Southwest itself. In the early twentieth century the territories of New Mexico and Arizona were, to most Americans, remote, alien places, characterized by a desert climate and unfamiliar inhabitants. They presented a picture dramatically different from that of the bustling cities and plowed farmlands in much of the rest of the country. Why, then, should the past of these regions be of interest to people whose ancestors came from Europe?

The way in which ideas about the Southwestern past and how to study it came together at Bandelier makes a compelling story. In piecing together the tale we are fortunate that the words of the participants in the early archaeological projects are preserved in letters, reports, and memoranda housed in museums across the country. One day while I was looking at some of these in the Fray Angélico Chavez History Library of the Museum of New Mexico in Santa Fe, the archivist handed me a pair of bound volumes labeled *Rito de los Frijoles Gazette*. Within their fragile covers were the single copies of the camp newsletters handwritten by members of the early archaeological field schools. Through accounts of daily activities, tongue-in-cheek news reports, and skillful caricatures, the *Frijoles Gazette* gives us an excellent picture of life along the *rito*—Frijoles Creek—in an era that seems increasingly distant. It also nicely illustrates the way archaeology, education, and identity came together there, influencing American archaeology and laying the foundations for everything Bandelier is today.

Edgar Lee Hewett and Pajarito Archaeology

Adolph Bandelier, who explored the region in the 1880s, inaugurated the study of the ancient Pajarito Plateau, but it was thanks to Edgar Lee Hewett that the region became a center of Southwestern archaeological research. Hewett's career spanned fifty years, a time when American archaeology went from being an esoteric pastime to winning acceptance as a full-fledged profession. Throughout Hewett's career the ancestral Pueblo people remained one of his abiding concerns, and his eclectic interests left a distinct imprint on the character of the archaeology of the Pajarito Plateau.

Hewett had begun his Southwestern archaeological explorations in 1896. He was raised in Missouri and came west as a teacher. With his first wife, Cora Hewett, he spent the summers traveling the Southwest and was captivated by the dramatic landscape of the Pajarito and its archaeological potential. Over the next several decades Hewett devoted himself to convincing New Mexicans of the impor-

tance of archaeology, using lectures, newspaper articles, and influential friends to generate support. Along the way he earned a doctorate from the University of Geneva and worked to pass antiquities legislation in Washington, gaining a national reputation.

From the beginning, Hewett's ideas about archaeology revolved around education. The second half of the nineteenth century was the time when "experiential learning," a movement that influenced many teachers of science, first gained popularity. In the 1870s and 1880s, field schools for the study of biology were established for the first time, with obvious implications for other research-oriented disciplines. During these years most archaeologists came to their profession from other careers, and many were drawn to field schools as a way to give their own students better training.

Because Hewett was one of the few nationally known archaeologists based in the West, his projects came to be seen as reliable opportunities for exposing students to fieldwork. His primary sponsor at the time was the Archaeological Institute of America, which maintained schools for the training of classical archaeologists in Rome and Athens. Hewett argued that such a school was required to teach American archaeology as well, and he used his considerable influence to make this vision a reality.

The Field School

Hewett's School of American Archaeology (later called the School of American Research) was established in the Palace of the Governors in Santa Fe in 1908 and was authorized to set up a new Museum of New Mexico on the premises. In order for the institution to get the best possible start, Hewett decided to return to the Pajarito and implement a new excavation program. He would bring in students of anthropology and archaeology from around the country and encourage public involvement.

Throughout the early summer of 1910 the *Santa Fe New Mexican* was full of reports about the new museum and the impending field school, hailing "the widespread interest of intelligent Americans in the study of archaeology." When work began in early July, headlines trumpeted, "Rito de Los Frijoles Is Mecca of Archaeologists." Over the next

Figure 14.2. Rito de los Frijoles field camp. Left to right: unidentified, Kenneth Chapman, Carlos Vierra, Kate Chapman, Frank Springer.

two years, late summer life along the rito moved to the rhythm of archaeological fieldwork.

Frijoles Canyon in the early twentieth century was a much more isolated place than it is today. Visitors took the old Denver and Rio Grande railroad, the Chili Line, from Santa Fe to Buckman Crossing, where they switched to horse- or mule-back to ride the several miles to the canyon rim. From there they descended by narrow paths to the creek itself. The only permanent buildings there belonged to the small ranch of Judge A. J. Abbott. A tent camp was set up for the field school, with the Abbott home serving as commissary. The ruins were close by, and many of the students and guests took up residence in empty cavate rooms in the cliffs. One tent served as a library, stocked with references brought up from Santa Fe. Space for lectures was cleared in the plaza of the ruined pueblo of Tyuonyi.

The field school was staffed by young anthropologists, many of them in the first stages of illustrious careers. They included John P. Harrington, who had already established a reputation for the study of Native American languages; Jesse Nusbaum, later a distinguished Southwestern

archaeologist in the National Park Service; Sylvanus Morley, on his way to becoming the most prominent Maya archaeologist of his generation; and Neil Judd, who afterward joined the staff of the Smithsonian Institution and led excavations at Chaco Canyon in the 1920s. Joining this group were specialists from other fields who contributed their knowledge of vital topics such as geology and botany.

The students were a more eclectic crowd. They ranged from Barbara Freire-Marreco, who had received one of the first degrees in anthropology from Oxford, to Maude Woy, a Denver school-teacher. Notably absent were younger graduate students from eastern universities. In the previous few years, some in the profession had come to regard Hewett as more a threat than an ally, especially because of his inclusive educational policy. In the absence of east coast students came visitors from across the country, all interested in archaeology and the chance to see it firsthand.

The Gazette
The *Rito de los Frijoles Gazette*, begun on July 10, 1910, chronicled activities in the Pajarito field school. "No pedantic accuracy will mar our scientific

Figure 14.3. Field school staff, 1910. Back, left to right: W. W. Robbins, Donald Beauregard, J. P. Harrington, F. W. Hodge, Edgar L. Hewett, Neil Judd, Maude Woy, Barbara Freire-Marreco. Front, left to right: Sylvanus Morley, Kenneth Chapman, Percy Adams, Jesse Nusbaum, Nathan Goldsmith, Junius Henderson.

reports—penned by the midnight campfire and in the haunted chambers of the cliffs," announced the inaugural editorial, written by Barbara Freire-Marreco. "They will mirror faithfully the impression made by half-comprehended information on an intelligent but ill-informed mind." Her witty observations about camp life were accompanied by notes written by other camp residents and the illustrations of Donald Beauregard, a young artist from Utah who was working with Hewett on projects for the museum.

One of the purposes of the gazette was to summarize the archaeological work that was the school's principal focus. Excavations under the supervision of Judd and Beauregard were conducted in Tyuonyi itself, while Morley worked in one of the cliff-side ruins, dubbed "The House of the Mountain Sheep." Work also took place farther up the canyon in the recess now known as Alcove House, where Nusbaum was reconstructing the kiva for future visitors. Among the artifacts discovered in Morley's excavations were wooden items described as "war clubs" and "one wooden sword stained with magenta dye."

The gazette offered written descriptions and sketches of some of these finds. The students set up a small museum in one of the tents, where they displayed artifacts for visitors.

Most of the actual digging was done by workers from the local pueblos, and their names and activities appeared regularly in the gazette. Hewett relied heavily on Santiago Naranjo, of Santa Clara, who had worked with him for years. Many of the other workers came from San Ildefonso, and they carefully negotiated the different requirements of camp and community life. The gazette of July 24 announced that the pueblo's governor had called the workers home for several days to attend to obligations there, and the work detail shifted accordingly. Freire-Marreco's diary describes men singing rain songs and dancing. Naranjo took her to Santa Clara to begin anthropological research there, which she conducted off and on well into the winter.

The routine of the excavations was broken up by a program of lectures given by school staff and visitors. Harrington's talks on linguistic subjects apparently were notorious, as one of Beauregard's caricatures suggests. Other speakers introduced the archaeology of the ancient Maya and Native American legal systems. Field trips to distant parts of the plateau, often led by Hewett, also invigorated camp life.

Like all students, those at the camp found ways to avoid assignments. The gazette reported that Nathan Goldsmith, a student from St. Louis, "enjoyed a pleasant little shooting tourney Thursday just above camp—unfortunately he was supposed to be doing 'Required Reading' at the

time. Developments are expected later." As in other field situations, food was a major concern, and even decades later Judd grumbled about the portions ladled out by Mrs. Abbott. One gazette notice read: "REWARD. 10 Bucks for the arrest and conviction of the guy who stole the pie & fudge from the Snake Clan." It implicated one of the museum's employees, Percy Adams, in the act.

As the summer of 1910 went on, many prominent scholars made their way to the Rito de los Frijoles camp. Elsie Clews Parsons, just beginning

Figure 14.4. Donald Beauregard's caricature of J. P. Harrington presenting a lecture.

Figure 14.5. E. L. Hewett leading a field trip in a sketch by Beauregard.

Figure 14.7. Frederick Webb Hodge by Beauregard.

Figure 14.6. Neil Judd by Beauregard.

Figure 14.8. Cartoon by Beauregard depicting Jesse Nusbaum, E. L. Hewett, and a summer visitor.

to develop a reputation in American anthropology, came through in August. The most prestigious visitor was Frederick Webb Hodge, chief of the Bureau of American Ethnology in Washington, who spent two weeks in the camp at the end of the season and went on with Hewett to conduct excavations in the Jemez Mountains nearby.

But it was the regular visits of members of the general public that became perhaps the most distinctive feature of the summer. The gazette lists the names of dozens of people who came, sometimes for a day, sometimes for weeks, to see the work in progress. A Mr. and Mrs. Nairn, of Connecticut, stayed for nearly the entire field season.

Toward the end of the summer, good-sized crowds could be expected almost daily, and even more came in 1911. Sometimes wrangling these visitors down the perilous trails into the canyon created humorous scenes, but they clearly illustrated the success of the school's public programs.

The pages of the gazette overflowed with these comings and goings. Gossip among the crew, under the heading "Blossoms from the Beanfields," was also a standard subject. Poetry was included, and when Freire-Marreco was absent at Santa Clara, others contributed different "editorial" perspectives. Occasionally, writers offered sincere observations about the school's work. "I wish to record the profound impression made upon me," wrote Frank Springer, one of the school's patrons, "by the scenes daily witnessed during my short visit to the camp in Frijoles Cañon…it may not have occurred to all who participate in the various activities in progress here that they are helping to inaugurate an epoch in archaeological science of far-reaching importance."

The culmination of the 1910 program was the meeting of the board of the School of American

Figure 14.9. Sketch by an unidentified artist showing a visitor inspecting one of the cavate rooms.

Figure 14.10. Beauregard's view of the opening of the Museum of New Mexico. The "Frijoles maidens" are Barbara Freire-Marreco and Maude Woy.

Figure 14.11. Agnes Laut's vision of the future Rito de los Frijoles.

Archaeology at the Rito de los Frijoles camp and the opening of the Museum of New Mexico's exhibit halls in Santa Fe. Newspapers lauded these events as major contributions to the intellectual life of the territory, and Hewett's students and staff played prominent roles in the museum's launching. The board, whose members included regional political figures and the famous Western booster Charles Lummis, ratified the school's policies and set the stage for future seasons.

When the 1911 field school opened, many of the original participants, including Freire-Marreco and Beauregard, were absent, but other visitors with artistic talent took up the gazette's pen. One of these, Agnes Laut, drew an extraordinary sketch depicting a vision of a future Frijoles Canyon swarmed by tourists and encrusted with cafés and postcard kiosks. This evidence that issues of public access and encroaching commercialism were pondered nearly ninety-five years ago, before a road even reached Frijoles Canyon, signals that our own worries are nothing new.

Indeed, the 1911 season marked the last time the original mission of the Rito de los Frijoles field school could be fulfilled. Hewett, restless, had begun to pursue other projects and for a time left the Pajarito fieldwork to others. His continuing feud with the eastern anthropological community caused him to rely even more heavily on public interest, eventually leading him to schedule the summer programs in Santa Fe itself rather than along the rito. In later years Hewett directed field schools in the Jemez Mountains and at Chaco Canyon, while the gazette, with its fond memories of the early years, slipped quietly into the archives.

A Field School Heritage

In many ways the summer sessions on the Rito de los Frijoles differed from the hands-on archaeological field schools run in the Southwest today. In

Here at night while the firelight gleams,
We gather around and each one dreams;
While Dr. Lummis with his guitar
Beguiles us with songs from lands afar.

Figure 14.12. Campfire at the Rito de los Frijoles field school, by an unknown artist.

other ways it is clear that the model for modern practices was established there. Even now, only a minority of students attending field schools go on to become career archaeologists. Most simply spend a memorable summer out of doors, learning about the past in a direct way. Hewett understood that it was through participation that people gained real knowledge, and the result was a better-informed public.

The heritage of the field schools that began along the Rito de los Frijoles is thus an important part of American archaeology today. It also reflects a recognition of the importance of the Native American past. When visitors to Hewett's camp returned home, they must have passed on tales of new discoveries, of grand vistas, and of lessons learned around the campfire. In a roundabout way this heightened interest helped to preserve such places as national monuments, and in 1916 Bandelier National Monument itself was established to include the Frijoles Canyon ruins and the surrounding countryside. Modern visitors, the successors of those who came to the canyon in 1910 and were featured in the *Rito de los Frijoles Gazette*, see the results of that work—but just as importantly, their very presence demonstrates the power of Hewett's vision.

James E. Snead was a member of the Bandelier Archaeological Survey and is an assistant professor in the Department of Sociology and Anthropology at George Mason University.

Times of Deer and Piñon, Turkey and Corn, Cotton and Obsidian

fifteen

Timothy A. Kohler

I was on vacation in northern New Mexico and driving south to Santa Fe when I decided to stop in the village of Chimayo to stretch my legs. I wandered down a lane past some decaying adobe buildings and abandoned orchards, but I paid little attention to my surroundings until I looked around and experienced an eerie feeling of recognition. I stood in the middle of a large plaza, mostly overgrown, completely surrounded by seemingly ancient adobe structures. The eighteenth-century Hispanic residents had built their village around a plaza to protect their families and fields from nomadic Indian raiders. My shock of recognition arose from the similarity of its plan—albeit on a grander scale—to that of the little village built by the Burnt Mesa Puebloans five hundred years earlier.

Thirty miles west of Chimayo, Burnt Mesa Pueblo rests on a high mesa north of Frijoles Canyon. I spent much of three summers directing excavations there in the late 1980s and early 1990s. The pueblo takes a curious form normally seen, prior to the Classic period, only north of Bandelier National Monument: four roomblocks joined at the corners in an almost perfect square surrounding a small plaza.

Burnt Mesa Pueblo was built in the late 1200s CE and occupied into the first few decades of the 1300s. It was founded during a time of great population dislocations in the Southwest and continued to be inhabited into the years of Bandelier's maximum population—a time of territorial behavior among the resident communities not seen during their first 150 years on the Pajarito Plateau. It has a small kiva in its plaza with some features that seem to connect it to the Tewa people. Though at most only two dozen households lived there, it was one of Bandelier's largest sites in the early 1300s.

This essay is a meditation on why the occupants of Burnt Mesa found it necessary to build what appears to have been a defensive village—and what happened after they did so. Although I briefly recount many of the findings detailed in the previous chapters, my approach is frankly personal. I offer my interpretation of what happened in Bandelier before and after these first villages formed and why the area was depopulated in the early 1500s. Data exist to support everything I say, but mine is not the only possible interpretation.

In the Beginning

Both the Burnt Mesa Puebloans and the shepherds and farmers of Chimayo drew on a settlement form almost as ancient as agriculture itself. Neolithic peoples—breeders of animals and cultivators of plants—began farming in the Near East 11,500 years ago, at the end of the last ice age. A few hundred years later they built fortified sites, such as the famous Jericho in Jordan, staking a firm claim to superior oases in a desert landscape.

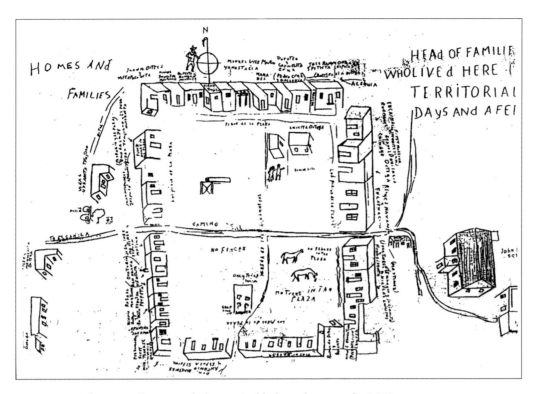

Figure 15.1. Sabino Trujillo's map of Chimayo's old plaza, drawn in the 1950s.

Farming developed later in the Americas than in Eurasia. The corn and squash so important to farmers in the Southwest were domesticated in Mexico by 4000 BCE and reached southern Arizona and New Mexico by 2000 BCE; beans were a later addition, appearing in the Southwest shortly before 200 BCE. The first farmers to settle in Bandelier arrived only in the mid-1100s CE, by which time farming was very old news in the Southwest. One of the mysteries of Bandelier is why agriculture came so late to the Pajarito; another is why it came specifically in the mid-1100s.

I think we don't yet know the answer to the first question, but it is a little easier to suggest why farmers arrived in the mid-1100s. From 900 to about 1140 CE, most of the Puebloan Southwest enjoyed a favorable climate, and a political and ceremonial system in which many far-flung peoples participated sprang up in the center of the San Juan Basin, at Chaco Canyon. The largest sites in Chaco Canyon, the great houses such as Pueblo Bonito, appear to have been built largely with labor contributed by these surrounding populations. People living and conducting ceremonies in the great houses relied on corn grown by farmers in outlying areas. Administering these activities was the job of a relatively small group of elite priest-warriors and their support personnel. But their control, or the population's allegiance, flagged during an unrelenting drought that affected large parts of the Southwest from about 1140 to 1180. To escape this drought—and perhaps the social chaos surrounding the demise of Chacoan control—some Puebloan farmers came to the well-watered Pajarito highlands, probably either from the San Juan Basin or from lower elevations along the Rio Grande.

A Time of Deer and Piñon

The Pajarito Plateau must have appeared to them like a Garden of Eden. Game, fuel, and farmland were abundant and there for the claiming. Hunting was probably at least as vital to people's livelihood as farming, and even limited resources such as piñon nuts could have contributed importantly to the diet. As Tineke Van Zandt discusses in chapter 6, the success of these early settlers is evident in their population growth and in the Pajarito's popularity as a destination for immigrants from the north.

The ancestors of both the Tewa and the Keres people likely were already living in the Bandelier

Figure 15.2. Burnt Mesa Pueblo, during excavation, with plaza in foreground.

area by the early to mid-1200s, but they intermixed relatively freely without having to mark their differences in obvious ways through ceramic style or modes of building their homes. Hamlets and kivas oriented toward the east or east-southeast are somewhat more common north of Frijoles Canyon and may represent ancestors of the Tewas or one of their close linguistic relatives. Hamlets and kivas facing south or southeast are more common in and south of Frijoles Canyon and may have housed ancestors of the Keres. But the frontiers between the two seem to have been open: the stone used for tools and the designs on pottery vessels reveal no social boundaries in the early 1200s. Residential sites are tiny and strung across the mesa tops in loose com-

munities of one or two hundred people. A few sites lie so far from any community that they might have belonged to none.

By the mid-1200s this way of life had begun to change, partly from the simple fact that after a hundred years of constant population growth and immigration, people were starting to bump into each other. This happened to hunters first, because deer are easily depleted locally and hunters must have ranged over large territories to find more of them. But hunters didn't just hunt; they also used their trips to collect resources such as chert for tools. As Michael Walsh points out in chapter 8, this is how we know that some hunters north of Frijoles Canyon began to be excluded from territories in

Figure 15.3. Tim Kohler (left) and Bob Powers inspect a stone ax from Burnt Mesa Pueblo.

and south of the canyon by the late 1200s. This territoriality marked the beginning of a new and more competitive way of life, which deserves its own designation.

A Time of Turkey and Corn

One hundred years of population growth had another effect on the rhythms of Pajaritan life. It had been people's practice to build their hamlets simply and stay in them for only a few years. When local firewood and game became scarce or field production started to decline, it was time to move elsewhere and rebuild—the old place was falling apart anyway, except for its roof beams, which people took with them. By the mid-1200s, available places to move to had become increasingly scarce. People began planning for a longer stay: they built with greater care and used their residences for a whole generation. With hunting territories circumscribed and local wild foods such as piñon nuts depleted, corn and beans became more important in the diet. Turkeys—which had to be raised and tended—also became increasingly consequential in the diet.

Now we come to a difficult part of the story. The late 1200s were a time of extreme turmoil

across the Southwest, and without more research in Bandelier and elsewhere in the northern Rio Grande, its events will never be clear. We know that the weather then was very dry, though presumably it was less so in the relatively high portions of the Pajarito Plateau (see chapter 2). Population in what is now Bandelier probably fell between 1250 and 1290, perhaps drastically. Curiously, there seems to have been no exodus of whole communities but rather a departure of some people from most communities. By 1300, when many immigrants appear to have joined the people who stuck it out through the late 1200s, the communities in Bandelier were no longer spread loosely across the landscape. Instead, hamlets forming communities sat closer together, with conspicuously unoccupied spaces in between. No hamlet stood unaffiliated with a community. It seems to have been a time of great competition among communities, and I believe isolated hamlets could not have survived.

This was the context in which a new type of settlement—the village, with fifty to two hundred rooms—first appeared, and Burnt Mesa Pueblo, though possibly founded earlier, is currently its best-known example. One impetus for forming these larger sites was probably the competitive, even hostile, social environment, in which larger groups gained a competitive advantage in defending claims to scarce resources such as superior agricultural land. Hence the defensive aspect of Burnt Mesa Pueblo.

The early 1300s marked the population peak in Bandelier. We would really like to know where all the people came from who nearly doubled the population between 1270 and 1310. One thing we do know is that high population densities forced people to rely more than ever on domesticated foods—this is when maize, beans, and squash became critical. Although rainfall was again sufficient for farming, other signs of a deteriorating way of life appear. Pollen studies and analysis of the charcoal from Burnt Mesa Pueblo suggest that the mesa tops were becoming deforested after a century and a half of heavy use.

Perhaps most interesting are studies of designs on pottery bowls from Burnt Mesa Pueblo and some earlier hamlets in and near Bandelier. These studies show that the number of different designs on bowls increased less than the number of households as people began to move from tiny hamlets to plaza pueblos with twenty households or more. If households were mostly making their own pottery, as we believe, then this suggests that potters in different households were deliberately imitating one another. Perhaps such conformity was reinforced by the close quarters in which people lived in these pueblos and the villages' inward focus; certainly one's activities would have been open to inspection and criticism by everyone else in the pueblo. This was a major departure from the previous 150 years, when families had lived relatively independently of one another.

I think this increase in conformity in pottery making reveals how villagers handled the stresses of living cheek-by-jowl. Conformity in ceramics was probably one symptom of a more general conformity to community norms. Conformity was not just a way of solving the problem of how to get along in close quarters; it also enabled these communities to present a united front in troubled times.

Conformity may help us understand a puzzling aspect of the archaeological record of the northern Rio Grande, which Van Zandt also discusses: how to tell immigrants from inhabitants. For a long time archaeologists have understood that many immigrants must have arrived in the region from places to the north, such as Mesa Verde, that were depopulated in the late 1200s. But unlike some other parts in the Southwest that also received immigrants at this time, in Bandelier the new arrivals decorated pottery and built households and kivas in ways fairly similar to those of the people they joined.

If we can extrapolate from a single case to the larger region—and I admit it's risky—perhaps we can understand why the immigrants are so hard to see. What might have happened in Bandelier is that most immigrants joined already existing communities that had recently dwindled in population. There, if our interpretations of data from Burnt Mesa Pueblo are correct, they might have experienced intense pressure to conform. And if these immigrants also felt that their religious system had failed them in the disastrous years of the late 1200s,

perhaps they were all the quicker to give up its trappings and adopt local practices.

Societies change, too. The famous social scientist Emile Durkheim described two kinds of societies. Those with "mechanical solidarity" are made up of many persons all doing the same kinds of things, who hang together partly because of their common experiences. It probably is not a great exaggeration to say that at Burnt Mesa Pueblo, as at all earlier sites in Bandelier, households all did pretty much the same things: they farmed, made pottery and stone tools, hunted, gathered wild plants and fuel, and conducted similar ceremonies.

The other kind of society is those with "organic solidarity," which hang together because people do different things and depend on exchanges to constitute a working whole. Once established, specialization forces cooperation.

Around the world, to paint with a very broad brush, societies of the first type have largely disappeared as they have been absorbed by societies of the second type, like ours. I believe the demise of villages such as Burnt Mesa Pueblo signals the onset, in the mid- to late 1300s, of a similar transformation throughout the northern Rio Grande, and so the last 150 years of life in Bandelier deserve their own name.

A Time of Cotton and Obsidian

The preceding chapters well described how the lives of Pajaritans changed from the early 1300s until the plateau's depopulation in the 1500s. This "Classic" period was marked by large, relatively long-lived population centers linked by trails. The largest villages, which I perceive as towns, contained large plazas and relatively few kivas. New ceramic types (glaze-painted wares to the south and biscuit wares to the north), new forms of rock art, and more craft specialization and exchange also characterized the Classic. This period, along with the years following contact with Spaniards, is clearly remembered in the Cochiti migration stories discussed in Robert Preucel's chapter 12.

Explanation of these changes, though, is harder to come by and often contentious. We all agree that new ceremonial forms arrived or developed in the northern Rio Grande region during the 1300s.

Many changes, such as the disappearance of small "lineage" kivas and the appearance of large plazas where public dances could have been held, were related to the success and spread of these new practices. We all agree that communities, centered on towns, became larger and that ethnic boundaries crystallized locally by 1300, and became broadly obvious in the distributions of glaze and biscuit wares after 1350.

Societies, however, are systems: when one part changes, others must as well, and it is often difficult to say which changes came first or were more fundamental. My suspicion is that changes in the Pajaritans' economy were as important in forming this new way of life as changes in ceremonial practices. Coalition-period communities in Bandelier generally featured little craft specialization or long-distance exchange. Kin and the household were the most important units of social structure. People treated close kin differently from others, but most exchange was probably of the type called "balanced reciprocity," in which households gave goods to others in the expectation of receiving roughly equivalent goods later. Such exchanges are as much about reinforcing social ties as they are about moving goods. Most of what people needed they made or produced for themselves, and so trade was more than an economic necessity. A society with this kind of economy also has strong kinship organization and "mechanical solidarity."

What began to break up this sort of society in the late 1200s might have been that lots of people moved into the northern Rio Grande who could not all be fitted into existing kinship categories. Perhaps they were lumped into the large group "foreigners," with whom unequal exchanges traditionally could be made. Communities grew larger, but reciprocity works best in small groups, and it began to be replaced by other exchange mechanisms. Finally, by the mid-1300s, trade with groups living as far south as northern Mexico and the movement of ideas along the now densely occupied Rio Grande corridor probably exposed northern Rio Grande Puebloans to both market economies and new religious practices. Indeed, the two might have had a symbiotic relationship, because the feasting and large public dances important in the new cere-

monial practices required special costumes and accoutrements that could have been obtained most easily through trade with somewhat specialized producers.

By the mid- to late 1300s, when Burnt Mesa Pueblo had become just an intermittently used deer-hunting camp, Pajarito communities were willing and vigorous partners in an exchange economy that extended up and down the Rio Grande and onto the southern Great Plains. In our limited excavations in Frijoles Canyon we discovered, at a 1400 CE roomblock southeast of Tyuonyi that we called Tyuonyi Annex, far more obsidian than anywhere else in our excavations. Most of it consisted of waste flakes from the chipping of obsidian bifaces, or "blanks" that could be fashioned into knives or arrow points by the end user. Interestingly, there were relatively few bifaces among the tools we collected. We presume the bifaces were made for export and ultimately went to trading centers to the east, such as Pecos Pueblo, or out on the plains, where obsidian was an especially scarce and valuable commodity. Sites in and south of Frijoles Canyon in Bandelier National Monument show particularly marked increases in relative quantities of obsidian during the Classic period, suggesting that Keres people dominated this trade.

From the Pajarito, then, came pottery, obsidian for tools, and possibly deer meat, hides, and finished cotton products. (Recall from chapter 11 the importance of loom features in the cavates of Frijoles Canyon.) From the Great Plains came bison and bison products. Corn, cotton, tobacco, and pottery from the Rio Grande Valley went in all directions. I think the large plazas in the Classic-period towns were used not just for dancing but also for trading. Whether or not that is correct, certainly more things, and more kinds of things, were moving around through exchange than ever before in the Southwest during the Classic period.

What happened to this system? What happened to towns like Tyuonyi? Ultimately, the Spaniards intervened, but the Pajarito was already largely depopulated when Vázquez de Coronado's expedition, the first Spanish campaign into New Mexico, arrived in September 1540. As Craig Allen points out in chapter 2, the years from 1400 to 1600 were drier than normal. Earlier, such conditions might have encouraged people to move upslope, but after more than two hundred years of heavy farming the uplands were largely deforested and depleted of game. Despite lower rainfall, settlement near the Rio Grande was attractive because irrigation and other water-management techniques made riverside fields more productive. Settlement in the valley also reduced transport costs for entering the burgeoning exchange economy. And so it was that by the time Coronado arrived, the Tewa people of the pueblos of San Juan, Santa Clara, and San Ildefonso on the north and the Keres people of Cochiti, Santa Domingo, and San Felipe to the south retained links to the Pajarito of memory, ancestry, and land use, but chose to live along the big river.

Timothy A. Kohler directed the Bandelier Archaeological Excavation Project and is a professor of archaeology at Washington State University.

Figure 16.1. San Ildefonso Pueblo, about 1912. The Pajarito Plateau lies in the background.

Two Pueblo Perspectives on the Pajarito Plateau

Julian Martinez and Joseph H. Suina

Robert Powers interviewed two respected members of San Ildefonso and Cochiti Pueblos and recorded their reflections on the Pueblos' connections to the Pajarito Plateau. He first asked Mr. Martinez and Mr. Suina to tell readers briefly about themselves.

Joseph Suina: I'm Joseph Suina, a lifelong member and resident of Cochiti Pueblo. Other than a few years away from home for military service and schooling, I've lived in Cochiti all my life. I'm a tribal council member and a former governor. I participate in the traditions, the kiva way, and I am also a member of the Catholic Church, as most people are in the village.

I'm married with five children, and I'm a grandfather of four. My kids are also members of my kiva and participate in the way of life at home. My family has been at the pueblo since its beginning.

Julian Martinez: I'm from San Ildefonso Pueblo. My name is Julian Martinez and I'm a native from there. My mom and dad are from San Ildefonso, lived there all their lives, and my grandfather and grandmother were Maria and Julian Martinez, who were well known for their pottery. They revived the making of pottery from the clay that's been found around our area, and my grandma especially was involved in some of the excavations that they were doing in Bandelier in the early times.

Being at the pueblo, I participated in all the activities that were going on for ceremonies, for our traditional activities. I also served in Korea in the U.S. Marines. I've learned quite a bit, from what I've been taught by my grandma especially. My grandfather was with me for a while, but he died when I was about eleven or twelve, so I didn't get to know him as much as I would have liked to. He was one of the elders who had big responsibilities at the pueblo. And so did my grandma. And my dad, of course, had some part in the things they do. As for the traditional ways, I still manage to involve myself in a lot of the things that they're doing now to help the young ones to carry out the traditions, the culture—to carry it on for the kids that are coming.

Robert Powers: Are there stories about the history of the pueblos, especially about what the significance of the Pajarito is to each of the pueblos, to their people?

Joseph Suina: Our elders tell us that we are in a continuing movement from north to south. And what we have in the way of traditions, our language, our ceremonies—all those things are what our ancestors gave us. Each of us, as individuals and as a group, is continuing that movement. I didn't realize that it was so literal until a few years ago, when we were building another HUD housing area. We were going to build some houses on the north side, where the ball field is. So we just checked it out with our religious leaders, our elders, to make

Figure 16.2. View of the plaza at Cochiti Pueblo, about 1880.

sure there was nothing in that area, sacred sites or anything like that. And they told us, no, you can't build there. And the reason they gave us was that we're supposed to be going south. That surprised me. So they approved the housing area on the south side, and a few on the west side, and some even on the east. So this belief, I think, is that the movement has always been from the north to the south. And that's the proper movement as a group. So actually we have a translation here into modern times. All the sites have been moving south and will continue to do so.

As for the ancestral Cochiti sites, our view is that you don't preserve them. We don't do what they do at Bandelier, where they pave and restore and all of that, for the tourists' sake. Our belief is that they're supposed to go back down to the ground—eventually, of course, the earth takes them

back. That's the way of human life. But at the same time, those places are now occupied by a higher form of life, if you will, the spirits of our ancestors. So those places are sacred in the sense that now they are not occupied by human bodies, human beings, but rather by their spirits. Their knowledge still exists, and their wisdom. Many traditionalists from home go up there to ask for that wisdom; tribal leaders might go, to ask for help, enlightenment on how to lead and be strong—some even go for getting inspiration for songs. So those places for us are sacred, living places. We still continue to visit and bring them offerings.

The Pajarito areas are sacred because that's where our migration originated; those are very important places as sources of understanding and inspiration. So that's one of the vital connections that we have that's really not captured in any way by archaeologists, in any shape or form. Of course they deal with one level of understanding, which is the scientific level. What I'm talking about is—well, to some extent it's scientific, but it also includes a religious connection. But I've been known to stoop to science from time to time!

In addition to that, those sites are the places we go to get our evergreens for dances, we go there for clays, and we go there for other resources for every-day use and for ceremonies. And of course those are hunting grounds for us—we go and hunt in those places.

Our connection with the past is living in that way. Like I said, we're a continuation of the journey going south. What we had way up north is still what we have now, and what we have now is hope-fully what our children will have. So this stream of living is not something that died there and is now gone, but rather the spirit of that life over there is still maintained through dances, ceremonies, and also through our attitude toward one another as Pueblo people. I suppose the lessons that we learned there in those places where people lived together in harsh conditions were the lessons that make our culture, our way of life. It is the founda-tion for our culture today.

So it's always with care, I think, that we walk on this earth, always mindful that there's an old way. Our elders tell us, "The old path, don't deviate from that." Yes, you can, you know, get experience and go out there, but you must follow the old way, and the old way is what came from the Pajarito Plateau for us. We're still doing the best we can, to follow the path. It's hard—TV and Internet, and all of that stuff of the modern world.

Julian Martinez: Yes, and video games and radio. In particular, you know that nowadays, when they're having the elections, they're always accusing us: How come some pueblos don't have women for governor? There's a lot of things [secret knowledge] that the women don't know, and they don't belong there. That's the reason why ladies are not involved in being the governor or the lieutenant governor. If that is to be done, you're changing everything, and we don't want that, and I don't think that'll ever happen. We've got kids who tell me, Why don't you get a woman? But once you break that tie, you're

just ruining yourself. The tradition is gone then. And we don't want to break that tradition. We won't expose ourselves to the outside.

Joseph Suina: In the pueblo, the first thing you learn when you're growing up is to take part, to be there, to help out, to share. And I think, now that I am older and know a little bit about the prehistory and history as well as our own personal traditions, our Pueblo traditions, I can see how the roots of a lot of our ceremonies and dances and our way of life are directly from there. That's what we're still trying to carry on, the best we can. I think I can say that the past in those places is present in our lives today, in spirit, in resources, in the landmarks, in relationships, and so forth. So we're all still con-nected today, in our real life, so they're not in the past only.

Julian Martinez: It is definitely the same for us at San Ildefonso. We have that same belief, just as he's saying, spiritually. The sites that are up there on the plateau, the Pajarito Plateau, we have the same feelings that whatever is there has been there and should not be molested in any way. Just leave it the way it is. So I'd say what Mr. Suina has said, we have the same belief. The spirit is still there, it's still protecting that place there, and it'll be there for as long as we take care of it ourselves. We're not doing anything to it. We're not going to put up posts there with notices that this is such and such. It will just stay the way it is now, and when it disappears, Mother Earth will take care of it the way it had been before. And the spirit will always be there, forever.

We will go out and ask for the blessings that they have. The spirits are still there, and that's the belief that we have. It's a strong belief that Native

Americans from here have, and I'm pretty sure it's the same in different areas—all the tribes, anyway all the pueblos, have the same belief.

What we find is that, spiritually, our beliefs and traditional ways are that somehow or other the people who originated anything there in the Pajarito put it there with prayers, and it's going to stay there and it shouldn't be bothered at all. And it's there for as long as you want it. And it's true, like Mr. Suina is saying, that we can go up there and ask, Can you provide me with a song, a corn dance song, or a buffalo dance song? or whatever you need. If you pray for it, it'll come to you eventually.

The Spanish people from the valley went up on top there, and my grandparents are the ones who helped them out, taking care of the plants up there. I believe you know, too, that most of the property up there belongs to the Spanish people, before Los Alamos was built. And that's what I was talking about, how they used to plant beans, corn, up there. My grandparents helped them harvest all that. That's about as much as I know about going up there to plant or anything like that up there.

Robert Powers: Are there any stories about the suggestion that there was a boundary in Frijoles Canyon?

Joseph Suina: I don't have any stories that really claim a line as such. I think our claims are more to those sites, those villages. So in the Pueblo traditions there isn't a definite claim that this is Keres and then that's Tewa. Instead, I think there's a more fluid view of place, so that I think there was a crossover, if there was a mark. I think the whole idea of territory is much more in keeping with later times, the sense of ownership of Spaniards and other European groups, Americans.

As far as a line, a Frijoles line, I really don't have any distinct stories or information from our elders about that.

Julian Martinez: I don't know, but I have a feeling that probably what really happened was that the leaders that we have followed up to now, in our traditions, that they set their foot down and said, This portion is for this, and this portion is for that. The reason why I'm saying that is, there's a story that a pueblo from that era migrated into Arizona to the Hopi mesas there. They are now Hopi-Tewa. Maybe

one of the spiritual leaders they had at that time on the Pajarito might have put a line, saying, This is where there is going to be a division. That's how they stood and now there's no conflict of any kind. That's what I think. Because if that had happened with the Tewa people who migrated to Hopi from here, maybe some other similar incidents happened up here. I thought that might have been what really happened.

Right now, we're working together in whatever we do. If people are poaching, that's not doing them any good. But if they had asked properly, saying, We want to go and do this, and given their reason, then they're doing it right. Their gain is when they're performing, and that's what their gift is, for them to get more.

The cave sites—what I think about those is this: the plateau up along where our reservation is has a lot of old ruins that have been excavated. Most of the pumice blocks are tuff, which is part of the buildings. My thinking is that maybe there were some families a little bit more knowledgeable, and they get a stick or some other tool and then start digging caves. So instead of building a house with tuff or stone blocks, they say, pumice is softer; why don't we just dig through there, build caves? Then put a shade on top there. They have their own little place to live in, plus any farming they're doing right below.

Joseph Suina: I think he's said it well, it was for that purpose, accommodating themselves to the material. It's probably a lot warmer—or cooler—depending on the time of year. Homes always seems to be on the side that gets the sun in the wintertime.

Julian Martinez: Meaning that they're smart enough to do that!

Joseph Suina: I guess what comes to mind for me is the fascination with the landscape that people who wrote had, not just its beauty but how barren it was, too, sparse in many ways. Rainfall isn't all that much and there's not a lot of big game, and yet those villages actually grew to a good size. What comes to mind for me is how those conditions connect our present to the past. The values that we acquired from them are the values of living together, dancing together, praying together. We still have that. It's amazing!

Connecting that with my other readings and my understanding of my own village, clearly the environment that was there, the hundreds of people that were living together in one place in close quarters in a sparse environment, suggests that those people had to develop a particular relationship with one another, with the community. It wasn't individualistic, you know. If people started hoarding stuff "just for me and myself," they would be in big trouble. I think that what has happened there on the Pajarito is what we try to exercise still today.

I mentioned earlier about joining, about taking part, sharing, and caring. As I sit here, I look at the dancers up there on the mural [on the wall is a mural showing a green corn dance, painted in 1931 by Oqwapi (Abel Sanchez) of San Ildefonso], and I think about how we do things. Unlike other tribes, in most of our dances we all dress the same, from the first in line all the way to the last, even the little ones. And we all—you've seen corn dances—we all shake the rattle together, we all move together. And the drumbeat, my grandmother used to tell me that's the heartbeat. That when you're dancing, you're aware after a while, she says, that our hearts beat like the drum, as one. And that's how we unify ourselves.

I think that probably our heritage which evolved out of the close quarters, sparse environment, came to us and today we're still trying to live that life so that the focus is on the group, it's not on the individual. And sharing and caring, being

there, taking part, is all still very important. And that's why I think for some of us, yes, we want our kids to get educated, but we also tell them, don't forget who you are. Come back but share what you've learned. Give back. It's not just for you.

I think all those things from the dances to our mentality toward the pueblo and to each other and all of that, and even the restrictions that it places on someone who wants to get educated and become an individual, it's hard to do that. The view on knowledge in our homes, I think, is that there's knowledge which is for certain groups, or for certain ages, or for a certain commitment. Because if you do become a religious leader, then it's for the people, it's for your life, it's for everybody, it's not just for you.

So that's why I think, as we sit here, I am uncomfortable sharing information. Part of it has to do with history and the way we've been treated, with forced Christianity and all the persecution that occurred. The other part of it is just the nature of our culture: knowledge is just not for anybody and everybody. Because you come to have knowledge—knowledge is power—you come to have knowledge when you're ready for it, when you're mature or you've made a commitment. There is some information that we just don't give out to people, and maybe that in itself has helped us to survive all these years. We were strong communities with knowledge that was kept within, which helped us to protect that. We're still trying to do that.

Notes to Chapters

Chapter 1, p. 1: "The grandest thing I ever saw…" from *The Southwestern Journals of Adolph F. Bandelier, 1880–1882,* edited and annotated by Charles H. Lange and Carroll L. Riley, p. 165. Albuquerque: University of New Mexico Press, 1966.

Chapter 5, p. 37: "In October 1913…" Elsie Clews Parsons's comment in Father Noel Dumarest, *Notes on Cochiti, New Mexico,* edited by Elsie Clews Parsons, p. 206. Memoirs of the American Anthropological Association no. VI, 1919, 139–236.

Chapter 10, p. 79: "They are not 'footprints on the sands of time'" and p. 85, "tell vividly and more lastingly…" from L. Bradford Prince, *The Stone Lions of Cochiti,* p. 7. Santa Fe: The New Mexican Printing Co., 1903.

Chapter 12, p. 95: "It is through the oral tradition…" Simon Ortiz, "What We See: A Perspective on Chaco Canyon and Its Ancestry," p. 65. In *Chaco Canyon: A Center and Its World,* edited by Mary Peck, pp. 65–72. Albuquerque: Museum of New Mexico, 1992.

Chapter 12, pp. 97–98: "Long, long ago…" from Ruth Benedict, *Tales of the Cochiti Indians.* Bureau of American Ethnology, Bulletin No. 98. Washington D.C.: Government Printing Office, 1931.

Chapter 13, p. 103: "The hardships have been so very great…" Coronado's letter quoted in translation in George P. Hammond and Agapito Rey, *Narratives of the Coronado Expedition 1540–1542,* p. 162. Albuquerque: University of New Mexico Press, 1940.

Chapter 15, p. 125: "Mechanical solidarity" and "organic solidarity" from Emile Durkheim, *The Division of Labor in Society,* translated by W. D. Halls, pp. 84–85. New York: The Free Press, 1984.

Suggested Reading

Allen, Craig D.

2002 "Lots of Lightning and Plenty of People: An Ecological History of Fire in the Upland Southwest." In *Fire, Native Peoples, and the Natural Landscape*, edited by T. R. Vale, pp. 143–193. Island Press, Covelo, CA.

Bandelier, Adolph F.

1892 *Final Report of Investigations among the Indians of the Southwestern United States, Carried On Mainly in the Years from 1880 to 1885*. Part 2. Papers of the Archaeological Institute of America, American Series no. 4. Cambridge, MA.

DeBuys, William

1985 *Enchantment and Exploitation: The Life and Hard Times of a New Mexico Mountain Range*. University of New Mexico Press, Albuquerque.

Kohler, Timothy A., ed.

2004 *Archaeology of Bandelier National Monument: Village Formation on the Pajarito Plateau, New Mexico*. University of New Mexico Press, Albuquerque.

Lange, Charles H.

1959 *Cochiti: A New Mexico Pueblo, Past and Present*. University of New Mexico Press, Albuquerque.

Lange, Charles H., and Carroll L. Riley, eds.

1966 *The Southwestern Journals of Adolph F. Bandelier, 1880–1882*. University of New Mexico Press, Albuquerque.

Lekson, Stephen H., and Catherine M. Cameron

1995 "The Abandonment of Chaco Canyon, the Mesa Verde Migrations, and the Reorganization of the Pueblo World." *Journal of Anthropological Archaeology* 14:184–202.

Post, Stephen S.

2002 "Emerging from the Shadows: The Archaic Period in the Northern Rio Grande." In *Traditions, Transitions, and Technologies: Themes in Southwestern Archaeology*, edited by Sarah Schlanger, pp. 33–48. University Press of Colorado, Boulder.

Powers, Robert P., and Janet D. Orcutt, eds.

1999 *The Bandelier Archeological Survey*, Vols. 1 and 2. Intermountain Cultural Resources Management, Professional Paper no. 57. National Park Service, Santa Fe.

Preucel, Robert W., ed.

2002 *Archaeologies of the Pueblo Revolt: Identity, Meaning, and Renewal in the Pueblo World*. University of New Mexico Press, Albuquerque.

Riley, Carroll L.

1995   *Rio del Norte: People of the Upper Rio Grande from Earliest Times to the Pueblo Revolt.* University of Utah Press, Salt Lake City.

Rothman, Hal K.

1992   *On Rims and Ridges: The Los Alamos Area since 1880.* University of Nebraska Press, Lincoln.

Smith, Monica L.

2002   *The Historic Period at Bandelier National Monument.* Intermountain Cultural Resources Management, Professional Paper no. 63. National Park Service, Santa Fe.

Snead, James E.

2001   *Ruins and Rivals: The Making of Southwest Archaeology.* University of Arizona Press, Tucson.

Toll, H. Wolcott

1995   *An Analysis of Variability and Condition of Cavate Structures in Bandelier National Monument.* Intermountain Cultural Resources Management, Professional Paper no. 53. National Park Service, Santa Fe.

Walsh, Michael R.

1998   "Lines in the Sand: Competition and Stone Selection on the Pajarito Plateau, New Mexico." *American Antiquity* 63(4):573–593.

Wills, W. H.

1988   *Early Prehistoric Agriculture in the American Southwest.* School of American Research Press, Santa Fe.

Index

Note: page numbers printed in *italics* refer to illustrations; entries beginning with an upper-case P refer to plate numbers rather than page numbers.

Abbott, Judge A. J., 32, 107
Adams, Percy, *114*, 115
aggregation: and late prehistoric period in Southwest, 43-44; and population increase during Coalition period on Pajarito Plateau, 46. *See also* settlement patterns
agriculture, *26*: and alteration of landscape on Pajarito Plateau by Puebloan peoples, 16-17; difficulty and success of on Pajarito Plateau, 27-33; evidence for transition to in Late Archaic period, 24-25, 37-38, 121-22. *See also* diet; maize; plants; sheep herding
Agua Fria Glaze-on-red pottery, 71, 75, *P16*
Alamo Canyon, 75, *P21*
Allen, Craig, 4, 126-27
Ancho Canyon, 65, *66*, 68
animals, and landscape of Pajarito Plateau, 15. *See also* bison hunting; deer; elk; hunting; rabbits; sheep herding
Applegate, Frank, 96
Archaeological Institute of America, 112
archaeology: chronology of time periods and major events on Pajarito Plateau, xv, 4; history of on Pajarito Plateau, 111-20; number and scope of sites on Pajarito Plateau, 3; and oral history, 95, 96; and railroad era on Pajarito Plateau, 106; and reconstruction of ancient diets, 35-36; and scarcity of Paleoindian and Archaic sites, 20; and Spanish in New Mexico, 104-105; and study of trails, 85. *See also* Archaic period; architecture; Classic period; Coalition period; lithic materials and sources; Paleoindian period; petroglyphs; pottery; settlement patterns
Archaic period (6000 BCE-500 CE): foods and diet during, 36-38; mano and milling stone, *18*; and transition from Paleoindian lifestyle, 22-25
architecture, description of Puebloan in Bandelier National Monument, 43-53. *See also* cavate pueblos; field houses; pueblos and puebloan peoples
arrow points, *64*, 65. *See also* dart points
atlatl, 20
Awatovi, 90

Bandelier, Adolph, *xviii*, 1, 31-32, 37, 53, 55, 79, 92, 93, 95, 96, 97, 99, 100, 101, 112
Bandelier Archeological Excavation Project, 3
Bandelier Archeological Survey, 3, 81
Bandelier National Monument: chronology of archaeological time periods and major events, xv; and historic documents, 103-109; landscape of, 11-17; and Puebloan architecture, 43-53; rock art sites in, 56-61; settlements between 1150 and 1190 CE, *P8*; settlements between 1235 and 1250 CE, *P9*; settlements between 1290 and 1325 CE, *P10*; settlements between 1375 and 1400 CE, *P11*; settlements between 1440 and 1525 CE, *P12*. *See also* Pajarito Plateau
Bandelier Tuff, 88
basalt: and geology of Jemez Mountains, 11; sources of and making of stone tools, 65, 67, 68
Bass Rivera, Angelyn, 7, 58
Baumann, Gustave, 55
Beauregard, Donald, 114-15, *116*, *118*, 119
Benedict, Ruth, 96
Big Kiva (Frijoles Canyon), *42*, *51*, 52
birds, in Bandelier National Monument, 15. *See also* turkeys
biscuit ware, and pottery of Classic period, 73, 75
bison hunting, and Folsom period, 21
black-on-white pottery, 73
Blumenthal, Vera von, 108
Bradford Prince, LeBaron, 79, 85, 100
Brody, J. J., 92
Burnt Mesa Pueblo, 68-69, 121-27

Cameron, Cathy, 98
campsites: and Archaic sites on Pajarito Plateau, 23; and Clovis period, 21; and Folsom period, 21-22
canyons, and topography of Pajarito Plateau, 11
Capulin Canyon, 32, *66*
Capulin Staircase, 83
cartography, and Spanish colonial period, 103-104
Casa del Rito, 45
cavate pueblos, *2*, *106*, *P19*, *P20*: excavation and interpretation of in Frijoles Canyon, 87-93; and rock art, 58
ceramics. *See* pottery
Cerro Pedernal, *62*, 65
Chaco Canyon, 79-80, 122
Chalan, Mars, 96
Chapman, Kate, *113*
Chapman, Kenneth, *86*, 87, 90, *113*, *114*
check dams, 28, 29
chert: and geology of Jemez Mountains, 11-12; sources of and making of stone tools, 65, 67, 68
Chimayo (village), 121, *122*
chronology: of archaeological time periods and major events, xv, 4; and cavate pueblos, 88; and rock art, 56-57; and trail network, 81
Civilian Conservation Corps (CCC), 108
Classic period (1325-1600 CE): archaeology and major events on Pajarito Plateau, 5-7; architecture and settle-

ment patterns during, 48, 51-53; changes in settlement patterns and social organization during, 125-26;
and diet, 39-41; field house and check dam, *29*; and
irrigation systems, 31-33; and planting of fields on
ruined villages, 31; and pottery, 73; and rock art, 57-
58, 60
clay, and raw materials for pottery, 72
climate: and landscape of Pajarito Plateau, 12-14; and
problems of agriculture on Pajarito Plateau, 27, 28,
124; and transition from Paleoindian to Archaic period, 22-23. *See also* droughts
Clovis period (9500-8900 BCE), 20-21, *P3*
Coalition period (1150-1325 CE): archaeology and major
events during, 4-5; architecture and settlement patterns during, 44-48; and diet, 38-39; and farming
strategies, 28; and pottery, 75; and rock art, 57, *58*, 60
Cochiti Pueblo, *40*, 95-101, *128*, 129-33
commercialism, and Frijoles Canyon, 119
community clusters: and large pueblos of Classic period,
52; and settlement patterns during Coalition period,
48
corn. *See* maize
Coronado, Vázquez de, 126
correspondence analysis, and dating of rock art, 56-57
culinary ware, and pottery, 72-73
Curtis, Edward S., 96
cutting and scraping tools, 65, 67

Dado, in cavate pueblos, 89, *90*
dart points, and Archaic period, 23-24. *See also* arrow
points
dating. *See* chronology
decoration, of cavate pueblos, 89-90. *See also* pottery; rock
art
deer, 37, 40, 83
deforestation. *See* forests
diet: and Archaic period, 36-38; and Classic period, 39-41;
and Coalition period, 38-39; and Paleoindian period,
36; reconstruction of ancient, 35-36. *See also* agriculture; animals; plants
distance decay model, and lithic resources, 67, 68
ditch systems, and irrigation, 29, 31-33
diversification, as agricultural strategy, 28
Dougan, Rose, 108
droughts: and agriculture on Pajarito Plateau, 27, 33; and
changes in diet during Classic period, 39; and depopulation of Pajarito Plateau during late Coalition period,
5, 47; and fires in Jemez Mountains, 15; and future
landscape of Pajarito Plateau, 17; and tree-ring record
from Jemez Mountains, 13. *See also* climate
Duchess Castle, 83, 108
Durkheim, Emile, 125

El Cajete volcano, 29
elevation, and agriculture in Bandelier region, 28

elk, *10*, 17
Ellis, Florence Hawley, 98
embedded strategy, and stone tools, 64
erosion: and agriculture on Pajarito Plateau, 27; and landscape of Bandelier National Monument, 16, *17*
Espinoso Glaze Polychrome pottery, 71, *P16*
ethnographic information, and reconstruction of ancient
diets, 36, 37, 39-40

Field houses, 29, 31, 45, 52
field schools, and archaeology, 111, 112-13, 119-20
fire, and landscape of Bandelier National Monument, 15,
16, 17, *P24*
fish, in Bandelier National Monument, 15
floor ridges, in cavate pueblos, 91, *P20*
flute players, and rock art, 57, 58
Folsom period (8900-800 BCE), 21-22
Ford, Richard, 74
forests, and landscape of Bandelier National Monument,
15, 16, 17, 124. *See also* logging industry
Freire-Marreco, Barbara, 113, 114, 117, *118*, 119
Friends of Bandelier, 80
Frijoles Canyon; view of, *P2*; Bandelier's description of, 1;
and cavate pueblos, 2, 87-93, *P19*; and depopulation
in 1500s, 52; and glaze-painted vessels, 75; and irrigation systems, 32; and rock art, 59-60. *See also* Big
Kiva
Frijoles Creek, 13, *P6*

Game traps, and trail network, 83
Garcia Canyon, 65, *66*, 78
gateway trails, 83-84
Gauthier, Rory, 5
geology: of Bandelier National Monument, 11-12, 80; and
cavate pueblos, 88; of Pajarito Plateau, 1. *See also*
basalt; chert; obsidian; soils; volcanoes
glaciers, and ice age on Pajarito Plateau, 12
glazes, and raw materials for pottery, 72
glaze ware, and social significance of pottery in Bandelier
area, 73, 75, 76, *P18*
global climate change, and landscape of Bandelier National
Monument, 17
Goldsmith, Nathan, *114*, 115
Great Depression, 108
grid gardens, 28
Guaje Canyon, 65, 66
guard pueblos, and trail network, 83

Hamlets: abandonment of in Coalition period, 45; and for-
mation of communities in late 1200s, 124; plan of
Coalition-period, 5
Hanat Kotyiti, *94*, 95, 96, 99
Hano (Arizona), 83
Harrington, John P., 68, 75, 95, 99, 113, 114
Henderson, Junius, *114*

late prehistoric period, 43-44, 46; and Classic period on Pajarito Plateau, 48, 51-53; and Coalition period on Pajarito Plateau, 44-48. *See also* campsites; hamlets; immigration; social organization; villages

sheep herding, 8, 105, 106, *108*

Shrine of the Stone Lions, 79. *See also* Yapashi Pueblo

Simmons, Marc, 96

Smith, Monica, 8

Snake Kiva, 90, *91*

Snead, James, 7, 8, 59

social organization: and changes in settlement patterns during Classic period, 125-26; and lithic resources on Pajarito Plateau, 67-69; and pottery from Pajarito Plateau, 71-77. *See also* settlement patterns; trade

soils: and agriculture in Bandelier region, 28-30; and landscape of Bandelier National Monument, 12. *See also* erosion

Southwest: and aggregation in late prehistoric period, 43-44; and katsina religion, 52; and study of environmental change, 11; and transition from hunter-gatherer lifestyle to agriculture, 19

Spanish colonial and Mexican periods (1598-1846): and archaeology, 104-105; and cartography, 103-104, *P22*; and establishment of New Mexico, 103; and human activity on Pajarito Plateau, 7-8; introduction of foreign animal species to Bandelier region, 15; and oral history of Cochiti migrations, 99. *See also* historical accounts and documents

spear points, of Early and Middle Archaic period, 23-24

specialization, and pottery from Pajarito Plateau, 72-74

Springer, Frank, *113*, 117

staircases, and Puebloan trails, 81, 83-84

Steen, Charlie, 30-31

steps, and Puebloan trails, 81, 83

Stevenson, Matilda Coxe, 100

stone tools, and lithic sources in Bandelier region, 63-69. *See also* basalt; chert; lithic materials and sources; obsidian

storage units, in cavate pueblos, 91, 92, 93

stylistic seriation, and dating of rock art, 56

Suina, Joseph H., 8, 129-33

Talus House (Frijoles Canyon), 59, 87

tempering materials, for pottery, 72

terraces, and agriculture, 26, 28, 29

Tesuque Pueblo, 74

Tewa: and ancestral ties to Pajarito Plateau, 7, 127; and cavate pueblos, 87; and oral history on connections to Pajarito Plateau, 129-33; oral history on traditional boundary between Keres and, 68-69, 75-77; rock art and ethnic identity of, 58-60

Toll, H. Wolcott, 90

Tonque Pueblo, 74

trade: in obsidian during Classic period, 126; and pottery from Pajarito Plateau, 72-74, 77

trails, network of on Pajarito Plateau, 7, 79-85

tree-rings, and reconstruction of climate in Jemez Mountains, 13

Trujillo, Sabino, *122*

Tsankawi Pueblo, 7, 33, *54*, 59, 67, 75, *80*, 82, *84*, *P15*

Tshirege Pueblo, 33, 59

turkeys, *34*, 38, 39, 40, 124

Turkey Springs, 32

Tyuonyi Pueblo, *9*, *50*, 51, 52, *102*, 126

U. S. Forest Service, 107

Urrutia, José de, *P22*

Valles Caldera, 1, 65, 66, 88

Van Zandt, Tineke, 5-6, *122*, 125

Vargas, Diego de, 99

Vásquez de Coronado, Francisco, 103

Vierra, Bradley, 4

Vierra, Carlos, *113*

Village of the Stone Lions. *See* Yapashi Pueblo

villages: in Cochiti migration stories, 99; and defensive character of Burnt Mesa Pueblo, 121-27; and settlement patterns during Coalition period, 48; size of during Classic period, 51

Vint, James, 6-7

volcanoes: and geology of Pajarito Plateau, 1, 11, 88; and soils of Bandelier National Monument, 12, 28-30

Walsh, Michael, 6, 77, 123

water: and irrigation systems in Classic period, 31-33; pumice soils and agriculture in Bandelier area, 29-30; sources of and landscape of Pajarito Plateau, 13-14

Water Canyon, 66

weaving, and loom anchors in cavate pueblos, 91, 93

White Rock Canyon, 6, 32-33

Woy, Maude, 113, *114*, *118*

Yapashi Pueblo, 99-100, *101*, *P23*

Zapata Mammoth site (Colorado), 21

zooarchaeology, 35